Mira Silverstein's
GUIDE TO
UPRIGHT STITCHES

Books by Mira Silverstein include:

FUN WITH BARGELLO
FUN WITH APPLIQUÉ
BARGELLO PLUS
INTERNATIONAL NEEDLEWORK DESIGNS
MIRA SILVERSTEIN'S GUIDE TO UPRIGHT STITCHES
MIRA SILVERSTEIN'S GUIDE TO LOOPED AND KNOTTED STITCHES
MIRA SILVERSTEIN'S GUIDE TO SLANTED STITCHES
MIRA SILVERSTEIN'S GUIDE TO COMBINATION STITCHES

Mira Silverstein's

GUIDE TO UPRIGHT STITCHES

×××

Exciting Needlework Projects, Patterns, and Designs Anyone Can Make

ARTWORK BY ROBERTA FRAUWIRTH

PHOTOGRAPHS BY SANDY L. STUDIOS

DAVID McKAY COMPANY, INC.
New York

I wish to take this opportunity to thank all those who worked with me in a professional capacity and especially Barbara Anderson who helped edit this book.

Samples finished by Ida Gold, Harriet Alonso, Carol B. Kempner, Mindi Kantor, Shirley Kantor, Elise Silverstein, Gigi Strauss, Joan Hyman, Mary McGregor, Eve Charny, Marie Gunther, and Jane Benson.

Diagrams on pages 110, 113, 118, 119, 123, 124, and 125 by Shirley Rose.

For Shari

Library of Congress Cataloging in Publication Data

Silverstein, Mira.
   Mira Silverstein's Guide to upright stitches.

   1. Canvas embroidery.   I. Title.   II. Title: Guide to upright
stitches.
TT778.C3S544   1977   746.4'4   77-10913
ISBN 0-679-50818-X
ISBN 0-679-50784-1 pbk.

10 9 8 7 6 5 4 3

Manufactured in the United States of Ameria

Designed by Jacques Chazaud

xx

CONTENTS

xxx

INTRODUCTION

Needlework is the general term used to describe all work done with the threaded needle, both by hand and by machine. It is divided into two main categories: utilitarian needlework or sewing, where stitches perform the basic function of joining fabrics; and decorative needlework, where stitches are used to create a design which decorates the fabric surface and becomes part of the fabric itself.

There are various kinds of decorative needlework. The most familiar are listed below.

Embroidery is a term most often used to describe decorative needlework applied to fine, densely woven fabrics, such as linen, silk, or cotton.

Crewel is embroidery worked with wool yarn or yarns of similar texture on compatible fabrics, such as linen or wool.

Canvas work refers to the kind of fabric used and not a special kind of needlework. Canvas is an open-mesh, even-weave fabric and the stitches worked on it will be a little more "patterned," or uniform, than those worked on denser cloth.

Counted-thread indicates the manner of workmanship when the design is not painted on the fabric but is reproduced from a graphed outline. The graph is counted in stitches or stitch units, and the fabric is counted in threads. The more threads alloted to a stitch unit, the larger the gauge of the design.

Surface embroidery is a figure of speech since all embroidery is worked on the surface.

Needlepoint is sometimes used to describe canvas work in general and the Half-cross or Continental stitch in particular. However, it is not a stitch. It is only another term for work with a threaded needle, or "point of the needle."

Creative stitchery refers to the most artistic form of needlework when the stitches are used to create an original design on the fabric rather than first painting the design on one fabric and then filling it in with stitches. Creative stitchery is also a general term for embroidery or stitchery. It is the art or craft of decorating fabric with lines and loops in interesting patterns with the aid of a threaded needle. The lines and loops are known as stitches.

The basic, or line, stitch is a straight line between two points and is executed with a threaded needle. The threaded needle is brought to the surface of the fabric, carried across it in a predetermined direction, then brought back to the reverse side of the fabric to complete the stitch.

The line stitch may be long or short, horizontal or vertical, or slanted to any degree; but in itself it is only a line. Worked end to end, the line stitch will, in some cases, form a curvilinear outline. However, it cannot curve or flex by itself without being anchored in some way by another stitch, in which case the line stitch is altered before completion. All knotted, looped, chained, and tied stitches are based on this manipulation.

When a number of line stitches are worked side by side, crossed over, or placed in any combination to form a specific pattern, they create what is called a stitch formation, or stitch pattern.

Each stitch formation has its own distinctive texture when worked over a large area. This texture is immediately altered with the slightest adjustment in the length and number of lines in the individual stitch pattern.

There are hundreds of stitch patterns in the lexicon of needlework. They are often identified by name and place of origin. Most of them are minor variations of a handful of classic patterns.

This is a beginners' introduction to basic decorative needlework. The accent is on the construction of stitches and stitch patterns that, once mastered, will enable the beginner to create a wide variety of beautiful and useful projects. Each stitch and stitch pattern will be outlined in step-by-step detail, and its special properties and usage will be explained. Many design projects are introduced in this book. However, beginners are encouraged to further diversify and explore, to invent new stitch patterns, to create unusual color combinations, and to alter, adapt, or adjust. The possibilities are endless.

XX

IMPORTANT INFORMATION FOR THE BEGINNER

Threading the Needle and Anchoring Yarn

For those who have never worked with canvas and yarn, a little practice is recommended before embarking on a large project. The best way to learn anything is by doing.

Read the sections on materials and supplies and buy a small piece of firm, interlocked # 12 canvas, a few small skeins of Persian-type yarn in assorted colors, and a blunt-pointed needle.

Cut the canvas into small easy-to-handle pieces, and cover the edges with paper or plastic tape. (Surgical and cellophane tapes will not adhere properly to canvas.) Even if the canvas does not ravel, the edges are rough and should be taped.

To thread the needle, fold the end of a strand of yarn over the needle and hold both firmly between thumb and forefinger. Pull the needle away without disturbing the yarn fold. Press the fold between the fingers until yarn is flat and barely visible. Press the eye of the tapestry needle over this fold and don't release the yarn until the needle is threaded.

To begin work on a bare canvas, pull the threaded needle up through the fabric, leaving a tail of about 2" on the reverse side. Hold this tail down with one hand while you work the first few stitches over it, catching some of the yarn in the process.

Subsequent strands should be slipped through a worked area and held in place for the first stitch or two. Don't use knots in

9

canvas work—they can almost always be detected. If a knot becomes undone, there probably won't be enough yarn to reanchor it, and several stitches may have to be taken out and replaced.

To end off the yarn, slide it into a worked area and keep all visible tails clipped. Tails will tangle the working yarn and the wool will shed a fuzz which will carry onto the right side of the work and become imbedded in the stitches.

How to Read and Interpret a Graph

The design variations in this book are based on a single stitch that is either vertical or horizontal. The first stitch and the stitch patterns that derive from it are explained in step-by-step instructions followed by graph outlines and stitch details.

Numbers indicate the entrance and exit points of needle and thread. The odd numbers show where the needle is brought up through the fabric, and the even numbers show where the needle is pushed down through the fabric. Once this is understood and the stitch construction mastered, there is no need for continuous step-by-step instructions.

The designs are shown both in photographs and in graph outlines that are read as counted stitches. The grid lines on the paper represent the stitches. The various line symbols indicate color placement, and a bold line identifies the lead line or the first line to be made.

FIGURE 1

Upright Stitches worked within a grid outline on interlocked canvas

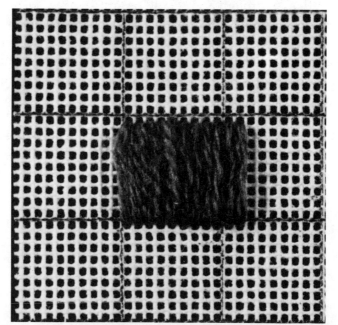

A graph is the skeletal construction of a design and is usually much easier to follow than a photograph. The graphs in this book are clear and accurate. The paper is ten squares to the inch; however, the individual design should be measured by the number of stitches per line and the number of canvas threads covered per stitch. For example, a canvas of four meshes (threads) to the inch will produce a larger stitch than one that has twelve meshes per inch. Most graphs are shown in half or quarter units. In the beginning, practice by working up these smaller units.

If a blank canvas seems a little confusing, make a grid outline by drawing straight lines *over* the canvas threads. With a ruler and a fine-point acrylic marking pen, draw the lines both vertically and horizontally every ten threads. (Figure 1.)

Establishing a Design

Design placement and starting point will be indicated with each pattern. Linear, or line, patterns generally begin at the top center. One half of a line is worked from the center to the right and the other half from the center to the left. Once the lead line is established, the rest of the lines follow, one beneath the other.

Geometric patterns begin at the center of the canvas. Fold the canvas in half and then in quarters, crease the edges, and unfold. Work a running stitch in and out along these creases to divide the canvas. Use a cotton thread in a shade somewhat darker than the canvas. This type of line division is more accurate than that obtained with a marking pen, and it will not show when covered with yarn.

Once a pattern is established, measure its dimensions to see how many units will fit across the canvas. Pattern units may be enlarged or reduced by altering the length of the stitches or the gauge of the canvas. A pattern worked over four canvas threads on # 10 canvas will be longer than one worked over four threads on # 12 canvas.

Practice one stitch or stitch pattern at a time. Change the yarn color or gauge of stitches for different effects. Keep tension even. Straight Gobelin and Bargello should lie flat and not be twisted.

Create a small patterns within the guidelines of the instructions. As you gain experience and confidence, begin to improvise and innovate. Keep a file of stitch patterns worked in different colors along with notes on the special properties of each stitch and ideas for future projects.

Your first needlework should be small and simple. Mount it as attractively as possible and it will serve as an inspiration for future projects.

Fabric

Needlepoint canvas is the most familiar of the background fabrics. It is an even-weave cotton fabric with open meshes that are easy to count. There are two basic types of canvas: single-thread, or mono; and double thread, or Penelope.

Mono canvas is a simple weave of single vertical and horizontal threads. (Figure 2, A and D.) It comes in stark white as well as a variety of colors and its smooth, flat surface is ideal for tracing and painting designs. Mono canvas is best suited for the Straight Gobelin or Bargello needlework. It is a standard, loosely interwoven fabric with durable threads that can withstand a great deal of wear and tear. It is recommended for large projects, especially those that will be used in upholstery.

There is a new interlocked mono canvas (Figure 2, C.) which features smooth, flat threads that do not unravel easily. It is an excellent choice for small projects. The interlocked canvas is not recommended for needlework that requires extensive blocking because the lightweight threads tend to break when stretched.

Double-thread, or Penelope, canvas is the heaviest of all canvases. For use in Bargello, it requires an additional strand of yarn or the double threads will show between the stitches. (Figure 2, B.)

A canvas of good quality is firm but not rigid. The mesh threads run straight and true, and the knots that re-tie broken threads are far apart and barely visible.

Freshly unrolled canvas may seem a little crooked, but a good tug at opposite corners should straighten it out. A very firm canvas that resists the tug may be relaxed by giving it a light steam-

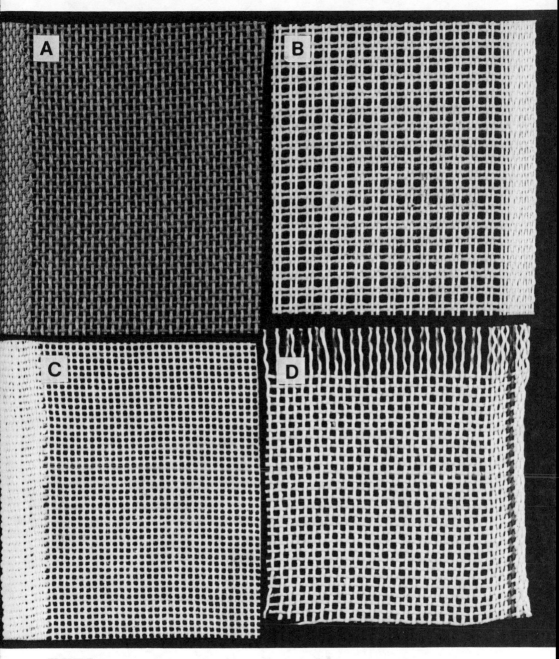

FIGURE 2

A, # 12 Mono canvas (interwoven) in tan; B, # 5 Double thread canvas in white (suitable for rugs); C, # 12 Mono canvas (interlocked); D, # 10 Mono canvas (interwoven) with raveled threads. Finished edges are called selvedge.

ing and them pulling it back into shape before it dries and regains its firmness.

Needle point canvas is always coated with a special starch called sizing. This gives it body and a firm support for stitches. An open-mesh cotton fabric would otherwise be limp, and the mesh threads would lose their form under the pressure of the heavy yarns. The stitches would look uneven and the over-all effect would be unattractive.

Starched, or sized, fabric is essential for all work that will require blocking. In the blocking process, a distorted canvas is pulled back into shape and nailed to a board. The sizing is softened by steaming. As it dries, it regains its firmness as well as its original shape. (For more information, see the chapter on blocking.)

Straight Gobelin and especially Bargello stitchery may also be worked on firm, even-weave linen. Some of the fine old Florentine work was stitched on linen with silk threads.

Needlepoint shops that specialize in canvas and yarn often carry a selection of even-weave linens for embroidery. However, beginners should work on canvas until they have mastered the stitches.

Renewing Canvas

After much handling, the sizing tends to soften. If the canvas becomes too limp, it can be renewed with a light steaming. Anchor the canvas face-down with a few push pins on a cloth-covered board. Place a damp towel over the canvas, and glide a hot iron lightly over the towel until it stops steaming. Remove the towel, and let the canvas dry for several hours.

For extra firmness, mist a little spray starch over the canvas before covering with the damp towel. Never apply a hot iron directly on canvas.

Mending Torn Canvas

The easiest way to repair torn canvas when working with upright stitches is to patch it. Cut away the ragged threads, and square the hole. Take a piece of canvas of the same type and gauge and place it on the reverse side under the torn spot. The patch should extend about 1" around the area to be repaired. Line up the threads perfectly, and pin the patch in place to keep the canvas from shifting. Work a few rows of running stitches through the two layers of canvas. Use cotton thread for this to avoid adding bulk to the patch. Press with a steam iron and let dry. If the canvas is not the interlocked type brush on a little white glue over the cut edges.

Work the needlepoint stitches carefully over the patched area.

Repairing Mistakes

If a mistake is noticed immediately, the stitches can be pulled out and reworked. If an error is made within a larger completed area, it can be corrected by clipping the misplaced stitches on the right side of the work with sharp pointed embroidery scissors. Pick out enough stitches to the right and the left to rethread a needle, and slide the tail ends through the worked area on the wrong side. Rework stitches. (Figure 3.)

FIGURE 3
Repairing an error

Renewing Yarn Texture

Yarn may become matted for a number of reasons. The strands look fuzzy and they seem to stick together. When this occurs, soak the yarn in Woolite and cool water for a few minutes and then squeeze the moisture out by running your fingers along the strands. Let dry over a towel.

Dyeing Canvas

Needlepoint canvas is available in a number of colors, but the most widely used are white and tan. White canvas is best under light-colored yarns, but has a tendency to show through dark yarns. If tan canvas is not available, tint the white canvas with a little coffee or tea. Simply dip the canvas in a bowl of warm tea or coffee (do not rinse), and dry flat on a board. Don't use very hot liquid because it will dissolve the sizing.

Household tints such as Rit or Tintex in creme or gray may also be used. It is not necessary to tint the canvas very dark—only enough to dim the stark whiteness.

Gauge or Mesh Size

Mesh is another word for canvas thread, and the gauge is the number of meshes per inch. A canvas with twelve threads per inch is sold as # 12 mesh. The more meshes to the inch, the smaller the stitches.

Mono canvas is available in a large number of gauges, but the ones most suitable for beginners are # 10 or # 12. Canvas with a gauge larger than # 5 should be double-thread because single threads will not support the heavy yarn needed to cover it.

Yarns

Needlepoint yarns come in a wide variety of colors and textures. The yarns used in canvas work must be strong enough to withstand the pull through the canvas without fraying.

Persian yarn is the most popular and practical needlepoint yarn. It is all wool and is available in an enormous selection of colors. Persian yarn is made of three strands (plies), which separate easily and may be adapted to any size mesh by adding or removing one or more plies. Subtle shadings can be achieved by blending two or more shades.

English crewel is also a multi-ply wool yarn. It is somewhat thinner than the Persian type and may require an extra strand of yarn to cover a given canvas.

Tapestry yarn is a four-ply twist that does not separate into single plies. It is excellent for any needlework but only fits some canvas gauges, usually # 10 and sometimes # 12. Pre-test on a piece of canvas before beginning a large project.

Rug yarn is the heaviest of all and will cover rug canvas such as # 3, # 4, and # 5.

Silk is one of the most beautiful needlepoint materials. The English silk is a little more shiny than the French, and it has a tendency to fray. French silk has a beautiful satin luster and is very nice to work with. Add small amounts of silk for highlights and a touch of elegance.

Six-strand embroidery floss is a soft and manageable cotton thread that comes in many colors and may be used to highlight small areas. It soils easily and should not be worked over a large area, unless the needlework is washable.

There are a number of needlepoint yarns made from synthetic fibers. They do not come in as many colors as wool yarns, and they have a tendency to mat after a time. However, they are washable, non-allergic, and often less expensive than wool.

Tools and Supplies

Needles. Needles come in a large variety of specialized shapes and sizes. They are divided into two general categories: sharp-pointed, such as crewel and darners for work on densely woven fabrics, and blunt-pointed (tapestry) needles for open weaves such as canvas or net. Needles must be compatible with both the fabric and the working yarns. Purchase them by size (gauge). The finer the needle the larger its number. Needles are distributed under different brand names, and although the eye gauge is fairly constant, the length of the shaft may vary. Find the length that is most comfortable in your hand. A # 18 tapestry needle is compatible with # 10 or # 12 mono canvas.

Thimbles. Thimbles are a matter of personal preference. Some needles slide through canvas so easily that it is not always necessary to use a thimble. But if you use one, select one that fits comfortably.

Scissors. Two pairs of scissors are a must: one small, sharp-pointed pair that fits into small areas to rip stitches or to cut yarn ends; and a large pair to cut canvas and other fabric.

Tape. Tape is another necessity. It should be self-adhesive masking tape available in hardware stores. A 1″ width is adequate. Fold it over the cut edge of the canvas to prevent the threads from raveling and to make the canvas easier to handle.

A **ruler** or measuring tape should also be part of your needlework "tool box," as well as some fine-point acrylic **marking pens**, and a small **magnet** to pick up stray pins and needles.

UPRIGHT STITCHES

Running Stitch

The Running Stitch (Figures 4 and 5) is the simplest of the straight stitches. It is the basic weaving stitch and is most commonly used for basting. The threaded needle is worked in and out of the fabric, covering several threads on the right side and several threads on the reverse side.

In embroidery, the Running Stitch is worked for decorative borders in single or multiple rows. The stitches on the face of the fabric may be the same length as those on the reverse side, or they may be longer, but the spacing should always be consistent.

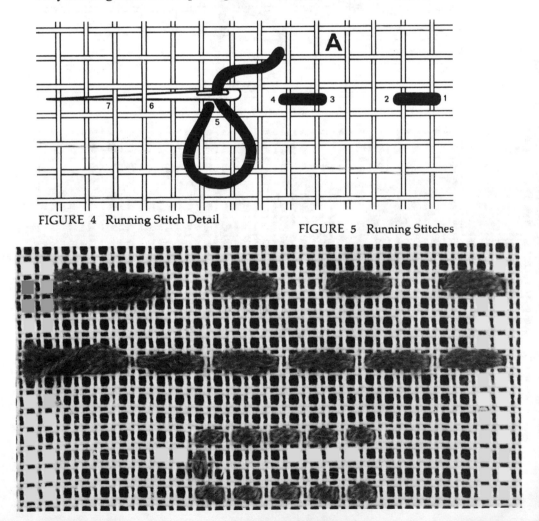

FIGURE 4 Running Stitch Detail

FIGURE 5 Running Stitches

Double Running Stitch

The Double Running Stitch, as its name implies, is a double line of Running Stitches. (Figures 6 and 7.) They do not run parallel to each other, but are superimposed. First, a Running Stitch is worked in and out of the fabric threads in a straight line. Then a second line of Running Stitches is worked in reverse over the first one. If the stitches are kept even, the row will look the same on both sides. Several rows of Double Running Stitches worked in close formation will create a smooth, reversible surface.

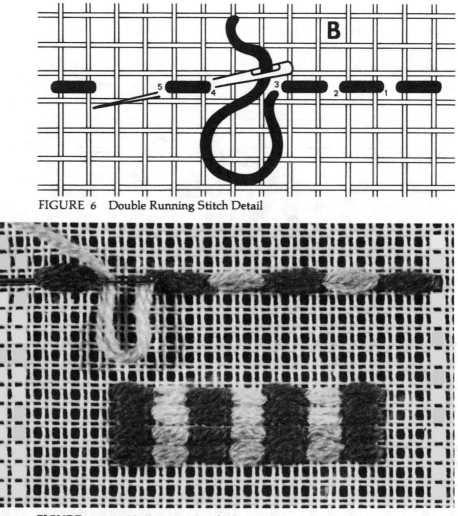

FIGURE 6   Double Running Stitch Detail

FIGURE 7   Double Running Stitch Variations

Back Stitch

The Back Stitch (Figures 8 and 9) is another all-purpose stitch used for general sewing as well as for embroidery. On the surface it resembles the Double Running Stitch, but it is not reversible. Come up at 1, go back at 2, carry the needle to the left under 1, and come in at 3 and back at 4. Continue in this manner, keeping the stitches as even as possible.

Although the Back Stitch is used largely as an outlining or as a holding stitch, it has an interesting texture when several rows are placed in close formation. (Figure 10.)

The Running, Double Running and Back Stitches are line stitches that may be used to advantage in curvilinear outlines.

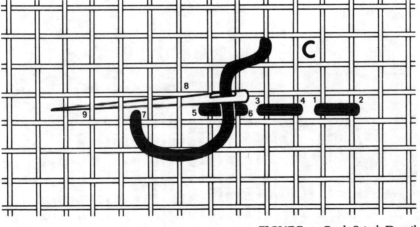

FIGURE 8 Back Stitch Detail

FIGURE 9   Back Stitch Variations

FIGURE 10   Back Stitch Variations

Straight (Upright) Gobelin Stitch

The Straight Gobelin (Figures 11 and 12) is one of the oldest and most widely used of the embroidery stitches. It can be seen in fine old silk embroideries of ancient China as well as in spectacular geometric designs from Sweden. It is the foundation stitch of the Flame, or Florentine, embroidery of central Europe and of the popular Bargello.

The Straight Gobelin is the basic line stitch worked over several horizontal fabric threads. It looks best on firm single-mesh canvas, and this is the only fabric that should be used in beginner projects.

Worked in close formation the Upright Stitch can create a wide variety of linear designs: curves, peaks, circles, ovals, diamonds, and an assortment of other interesting shapes.

The next few chapters will illustrate the properties and design progressions of the Straight Gobelin, or Upright Stitch.

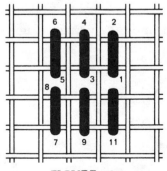

FIGURE 11
Straight Gobelin Stitch

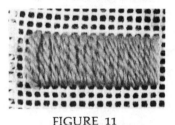

FIGURE 12
Straight Gobelin Stitch Detail

Straight Gobelin—Ribbed Texture

The Straight Gobelin Stitch worked in close formation will create even horizontal rows or a ribbed texture. The length of stitches may vary in alternate rows but should be of equal size within an individual row.

A ribbed texture in its simplest form translates into stripes. Colors may be changed for every second row or worked in a number of bright colors and repeated as often as the project allows.

Wider bands of color are created by working two or more adjacent rows in the same color or by increasing the length of stitches in a single row. Colors may be changed within a row to achieve some very interesting designs such as the abstract on page 27 and the gingham on page 26.

Ribbing may be worked over two or more canvas threads. It does not work too well over one thread because the stitches seem to disappear into the canvas. When a narrow line of stitches is desired, it may be worked up over a line of trame as follows: Knot a matching strand of yarn somewhat longer than the proposed row. Carry the yarn across the face of the canvas parallel to the horizontal canvas thread to be covered and fasten it at the other end. With a second strand of yarn in matching color, work a line of small straight stitches over the trame strand and the single canvas thread. Guide the trame strand and keep it taut as you work. Clip both ends of trame. (Figure 13.)

Rows of Straight Gobelin Stitches should be worked with an even tension. If the canvas shows a gap between the stitch lines, go over it with a line of Back Stitches. Make these more decorative by using shiny cotton embroidery floss. (Figure 14.)

FIGURE 13 Trame Stitch Detail

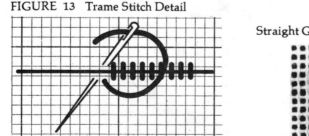

FIGURE 14
Straight Gobelin with Back Stitch

Abstract Design with Ribbed Texture

To create an abstract design work with black and white or any two compatible colors. (Figures 16 and 17.) Thread two needles and begin working from the top. The bold lines on the graph indicate the darker tone. Stitch each horizontal row, changing colors as indicated. The rows alternate from two canvas threads to five. When you reach the bottom of the graph pattern, repeat from the top.

Working with two threaded needles is not difficult, and it eliminates the need to cut and fasten so many threads. As you finish one color, fasten the needle above or below the work line until it is needed again. Then bring the threaded needle under the worked stitches and back into position. (Figure 15.)

FIGURE 15
Working Upright Stitch in two colors

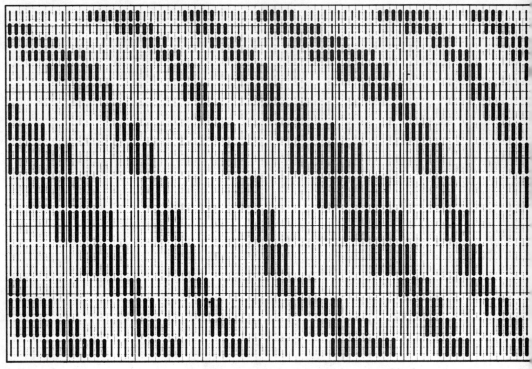

FIGURE 16 Abstract Design in Straight Gobelin showing ribbed texture

Gingham

The Gingham pattern (Figure 18) is based on alternating squares of dark, medium, and light colors. In the first row, alternate white and medium. In the second row, alternate medium and dark. The squares, worked in Straight Gobelin, consist of six stitches worked over six canvas threads.

FIGURE 18
Gingham pattern worked
in Upright Stitch

FIGURE 17 Abstract Design in Straight Gobelin showing ribbed texture

Diagonal Rows

The straight Gobelin Stitch may be used to create diagonal rows. Instead of working in close formation, raise each stitch by one canvas thread and work a diagonal row of stitches upward and downward. (Figure 19.) This technique adapts to many interesting patterns. (Figures 20, 21, 22, and 23.) The bolder rows should be worked first; they form the outline of the pattern.

Figure 24 shows a repeat pattern of small units worked in bright colors. Each unit begins with a vertical stitch over seven canvas threads. Notice the outline of the wider framework and the second inner frame, which is narrow and placed over two threads. The

FIGURE 19
Diagonal Lines worked in Upright Stitch

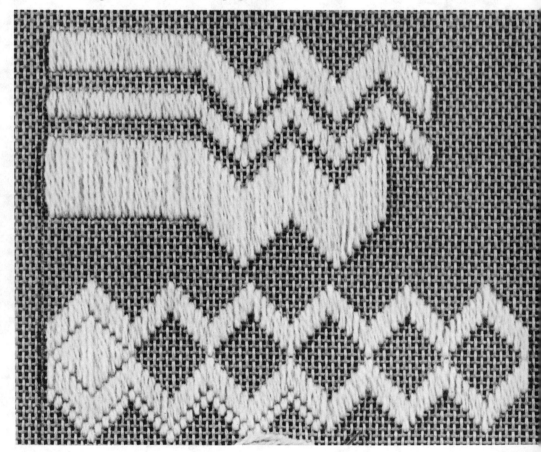

center is a diamond worked over the remaining threads. Finish the pattern units first, changing colors at random. This is a good way to use up leftover strands of yarn. The spaces left between the pattern units are filled in crosswise. The dark color creates a background and unifies the design. (Figure 25 and color page C2.)

Figure 26 is an adaptation from an antique patchwork quilt called "monkeywrench." Each pattern unit is a series of triangles and diamonds. The units interlock. Work up the first unit in the center of the canvas. This will establish the design and give you an idea of how much yarn and how many units are needed for the over-all project. This design looks best in two colors or one color plus white. (Figure 27.)

Figure 28 shows a series of diamond units worked in horizontal rows in changing colors. Make this in any size or color combination. The two small purses on color page C1 are one pattern worked in two color schemes.

FIGURE 20
Pattern variations worked in Upright Stitch

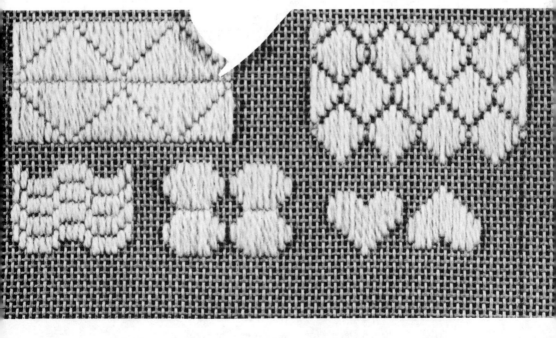

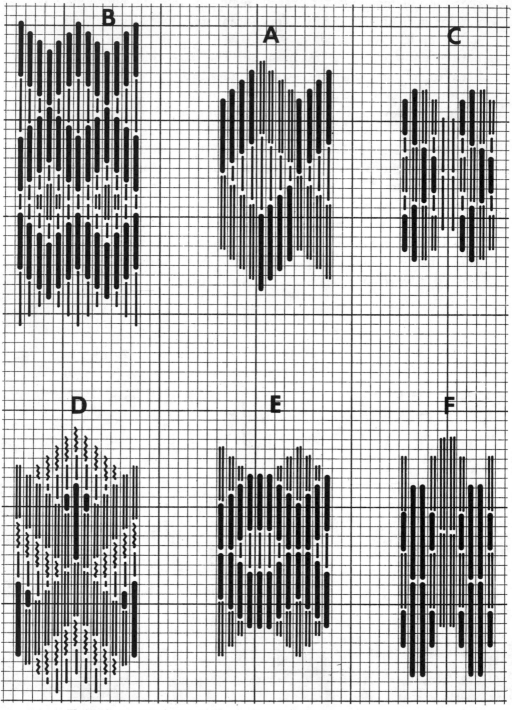

FIGURE 21 Stitch Details for small patterns in Figure 22

FIGURE 22
Small patterns worked in Upright Stitch

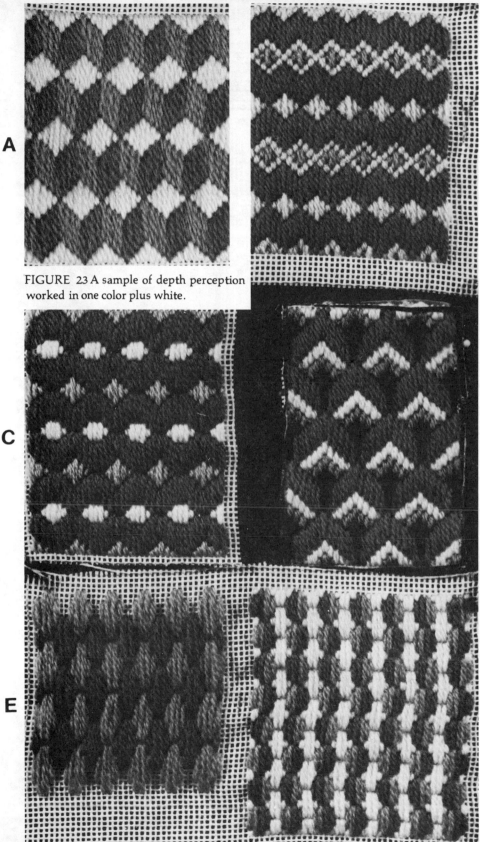

FIGURE 23 A sample of depth perception worked in one color plus white.

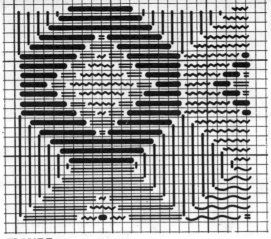

FIGURE 24

Stitch Detail for small repeat patterns worked
in assorted colors (see color page C2, Bottom, C).

FIGURE 28

Stitch detail for two small handbags
(shown in two color schemes on
color page C1, Top, A).

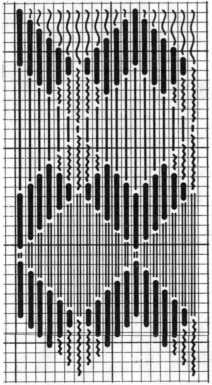

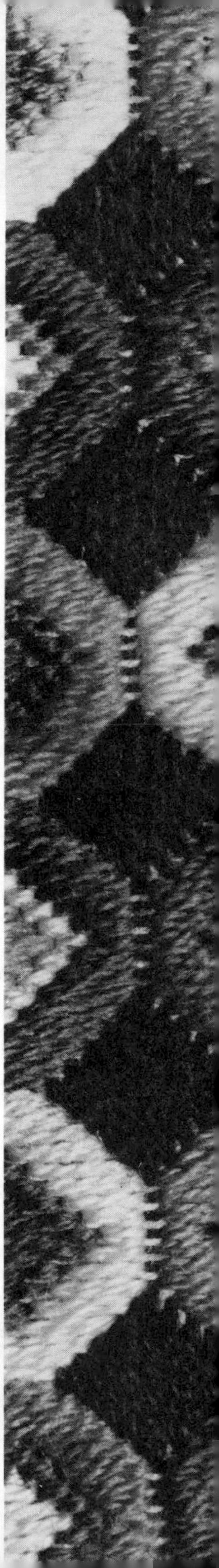

FIGURE 25

Stitch Detail for small repeat
patterns worked in assorted colors
(see color page C2, Bottom, C).

FIGURE 26
Stitch Detail for Monkeywrench pattern in two colors

FIGURE 27
Monkeywrench Pattern (adaptation from antique patchwork quilt)

Brick Stitch

The Brick Stitch (Figure 29) is a series of Straight Gobelin Stitches worked over an even number of canvas threads and placed in staggered rows like bricks.

The Brick Stitch is not a stitch *pattern*; that is there is no block or unit of stitches that can be singled out as a Brick Stitch pattern. It is rather a special method or technique of stitch placement which creates a distinctive texture.

In the first row, a space is skipped between each stitch. In the second row the stitches are placed in the empty spaces at the half mark so that the rows interlock. The Brick Stitch is easier to work than the ribbed lines of the Straight Gobelin, and it is a good choice for a flat background.

The best way to show off the brick stitch is in stripes. The rows of interlocking stitches create a saw-tooth line that may be used in a number of color variations on anything from an eyeglass case to a rug.

The small rug in Figure 30 is worked on heavy # 4 canvas with double strands of rug yarn in several shades of green. The stitches are placed over four strands of canvas and worked from left to right and right to left.

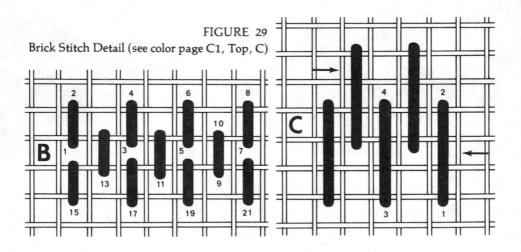

FIGURE 29
Brick Stitch Detail (see color page C1, Top, C)

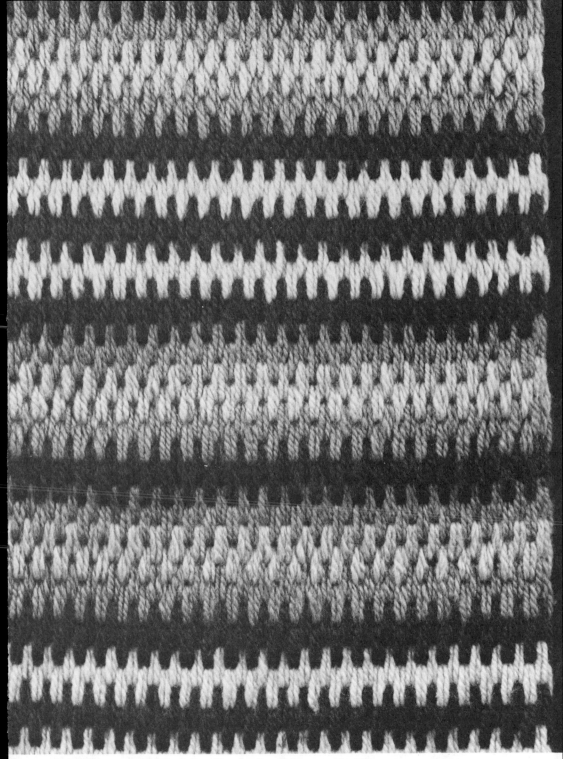

FIGURE 30   Brick Stitch Rug Pattern (see color page C4, B)

The small dollhouse rug on color page C4 measures 6" × 9" and is worked in Brick Stitch in random stripes of magenta, purple, orange, and green. Fringes may be bought in stores that sell trimmings and notions.

The eyeglass case on color page C1 is worked in Double Brick Stitch (two stitches over two spaces in each row instead of single stitches). Directions for finishing the eyeglass case are on pages 119-120.

A large number of Bargello designs and outlines are worked within the framework of the Brick Stitch texture. Study Figure 31. The Brick Stitch format is shown in the way the stitches relate to one another.

A horizontal row is a series of spaced line stitches, a vertical line places the stitches one below the other, and a diagonal line consists of steps raised over two canvas strands. (Figure 32.)

One of the best examples is the Bargello carnation pattern. The carnation is worked in two shades of pink plus green on a white background. Study the pattern construction in Figure 33. Notice the Brick Stitch framework in steps A and B in the first two color placements. In step C, the completed carnation fits perfectly within the background. (See Figures 34 and 35 and color page C2.) The carnation may be altered slightly by rearranging the color sequence.

When creating a design outline in Brick Stitch, do not work from opposite ends of the canvas or the stitches may not align when they reach the middle. Build the design from one point, and place each stitch adjacent to the previous one. To space pattern units such as the carnation, finish one unit and connect it to the others with a horizontal or vertical line of background Brick Stitches. Begin a second unit at the end of that line.

In Figures 36, 37, and 38 are several examples of patterns that can be created with the brick stitch.

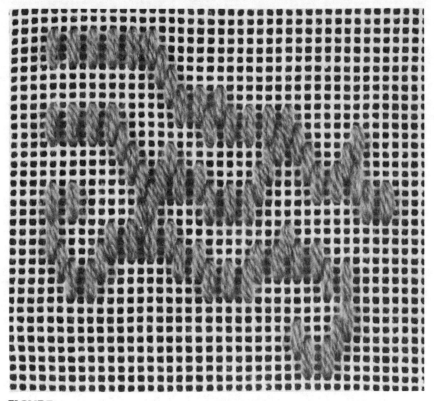

FIGURE 31
Brick Stitch format showing the way the stitches relate to one another

FIGURE 32
Upright Stitches worked in steps,
worked over two canvas strands

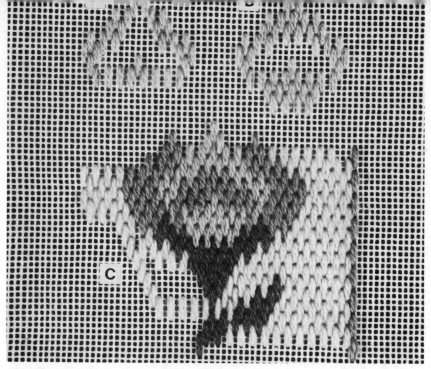

FIGURE 33

The completed carnation fits perfectly within the Brick Stitch background (see color page C2, Top, D).

FIGURE 34

Carnation Pattern Stitch Detail (see color page C2, Top, D)

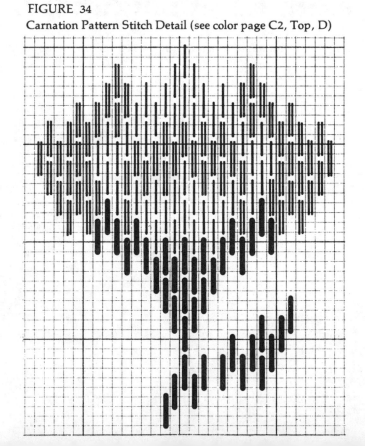

FIGURE 35 Carnations in an over-all design (see color page C2, Top, D)

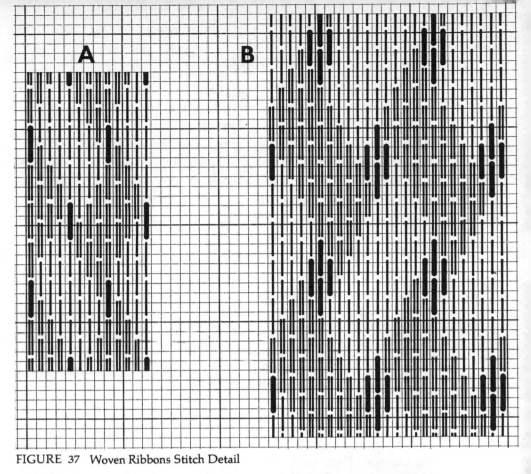

FIGURE 37 Woven Ribbons Stitch Detail

FIGURE 38 Woven Ribbons

FIGURE 36

Parisian Stitch Texture

The Parisian Stitch texture (Figure 39) is a series of large and small stitches worked in sequence. It can be identified only as a texture and not as an individual stitch pattern.

The Parisian Stitch texture appears to be a three-stitch unit—a long stitch flanked by two short ones—but it is always worked as a continuous row of evenly spaced long and short stitches. Usually the short stitch is taken over two canvas threads and the long stitch over four threads. The short stitches are centered between the long ones.

To create the Parisian Stitch texture, come up at 1, bring the needle back at 2, and continue working over and under the canvas from right to left or left to right.

Figure 40 illustrates the relation of the stitches to one another horizontally, vertically, diagonally, and in free-form outline. When creating a design outline within the Parisian Stitch texture, work with the larger stitches first, following the guidelines in the photo. Place all the smaller stitches at one time. Vary the colors as needed, or place small beads in the space allowance for the smaller stitch. The Parisian Stitch texture can be used to create interesting backgrounds and to fill small patchwork areas. It will not distort the canvas. (Figures 41 and 42.)

FIGURE 39

Parisian Stitch Detail

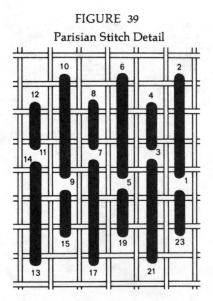

FIGURE 40

Parisian Stitch Variations

FIGURE 41 Parisian Stitch in two colors

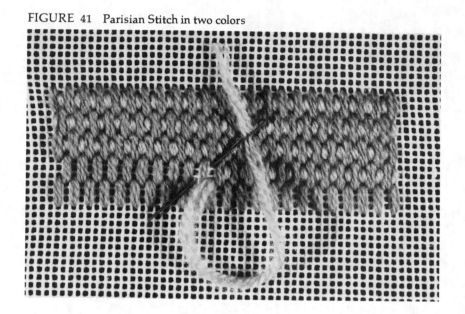

FIGURE 42 Parisian Stitch Stripes

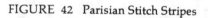

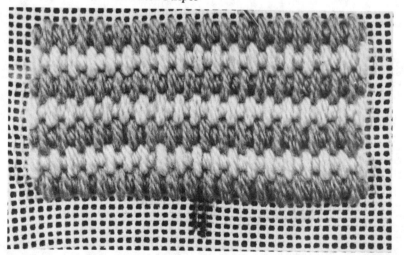

Hungarian Stitch Pattern

The Hungarian Stitch pattern (Figures 43, 44, and 45) is a combination of three Upright Stitches—one long and two short on either side. It looks exactly like the Parisian Stitch pattern and is worked in the same sequence of one short, one long, one short. But while the Parisian is worked in a continuous row, the Hungarian is worked by skipping a space between the stitch patterns so that they become clearly visible as individual units.

The Hungarian is one of the smallest stitch patterns as well as one of the most versatile. It may be used for small areas, bold patterns, and backgrounds. It also lends itself to attractive pattern variations. (Figures 46, 47, 48, and 49.)

As shown in the graph outline, the Hungarian Stitch is worked from left to right or right to left. The needle goes in at odd numbers and comes out at even numbers. The variations are slightly larger versions of the pattern. The Hungarian Stitch formation is evident by the open space between the diamonds. Once the open space is covered with an extra stitch, it is no longer a Hungerian Stitch pattern but a diamond pattern.

Figure 50 shows an interesting project that can be worked with the Hungarian Stitch pattern.

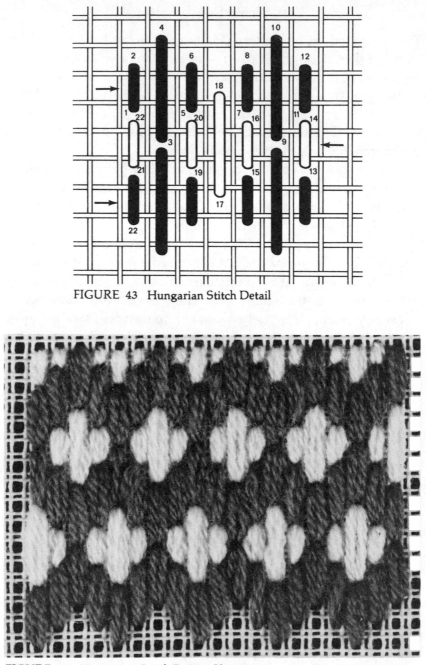

FIGURE 43 Hungarian Stitch Detail

FIGURE 44 Hungarian Stitch Pattern Variations

FIGURE 45
Hungarian Stitch Pattern Variations

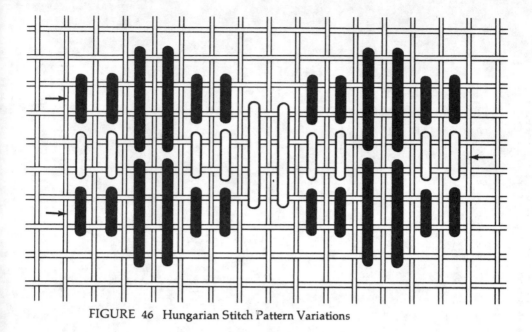

FIGURE 46 Hungarian Stitch Pattern Variations

FIGURE 47 Double Hungarian Stitch Variation

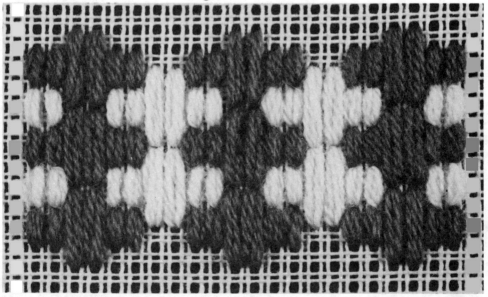

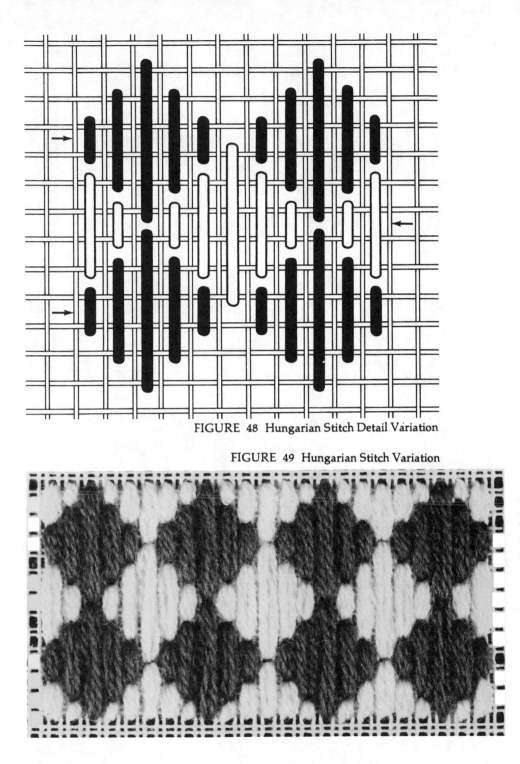

FIGURE 48 Hungarian Stitch Detail Variation

FIGURE 49 Hungarian Stitch Variation

FIGURE 50

Diamond Stitch Pattern

The Diamond Stitch pattern (Figure 51) is the most familiar of the Upright Stitch patterns. It is worked like a double triangle. The stitches are raised by one canvas thread both upward and downward from the first stitch. The progression is 1–3–5–7 or more stitches and back to the original single stitch.

When a stitch is skipped between the diamond units, a variation of the Hungarian Stitch pattern is created. When the first (smallest) stitch links the diamond units without leaving a space in between, the alternate rows of diamonds will be slightly smaller.

Figure 52 shows an interesting diamond variation made using the Hungarian Stitch pattern. Work from right to left on the top row, and from left to right on the next row, continuing until the desired number of rows is completed. Then simply turn the canvas and fill in the spaces with more of the Hungarian Stitch pattern.

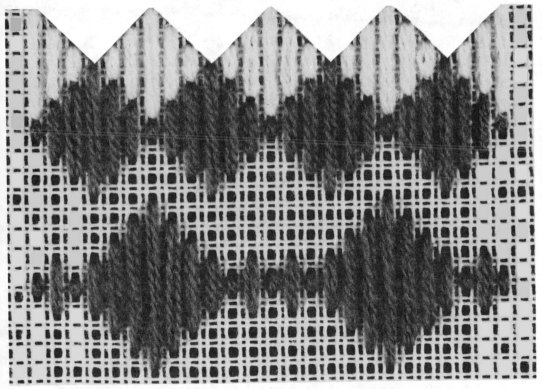

FIGURE 51 Diamond Stitch Pattern and Variation

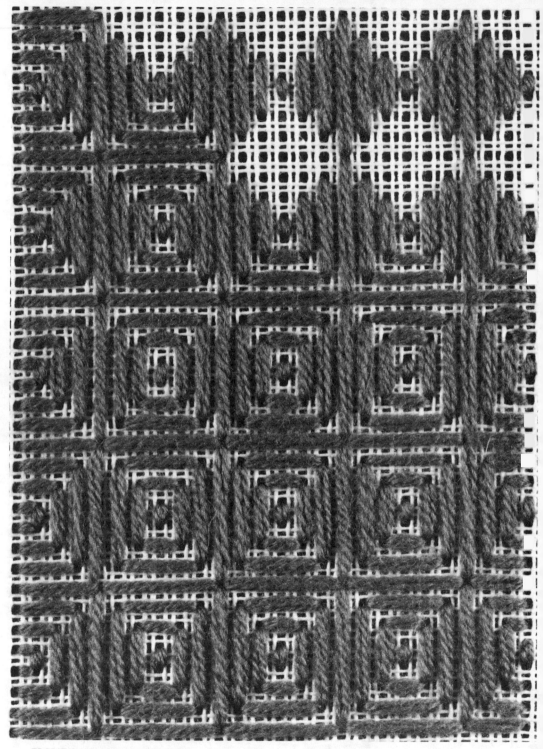

FIGURE 52 Diamond Stitch Patterns worked horizontally and vertically to create an unusual over-all design. Stitch progression shown at upper right.

Triangle Stitch Patterns

Triangles are made up of Straight Gobelin Stitches raised by one canvas thread beginning with one stitch over one canvas thread and continuing over 2–3–4–5–4–3–2–1. By increasing or decreasing the length of the longest stitch, the triangle can be made larger or smaller. The stitches are lengthened at the top line only; the bottom line remains constant.

Triangles can be worked in interesting geometric patterns or angled four ways to create large squares. (Figures 53, 54, and 55.) Work carefully on firm canvas. If the stitches are pulled too tightly, the canvas threads will separate, causing unattractive gaps as in Figure 54.

Triangle units are also created with step progressions worked over two canvas threads. These are worked over 2–4–6–4–2, 2–4–6 –8–6–4–2, etc. canvas threads. These triangles fit into hexagons, trapeziums, parallelograms, and six-point stars as shown in Figures 56, 57, and 58.

Triangles in primary and secondary colors (color page C2) are worked over one to ten canvas threads and back to one.

FIGURE 53 Triangle Stitch Detail

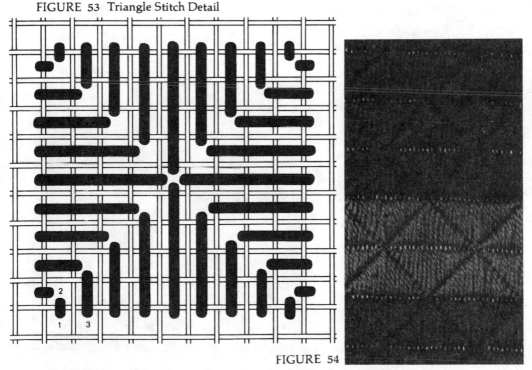

FIGURE 54

Triangles in primary and secondary colors. Each triangle is worked over one to ten canvas threads and back to one (see color page C2, Bottom, B).

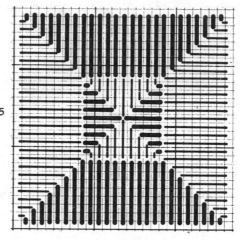

FIGURE 55

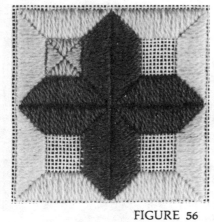

FIGURE 56

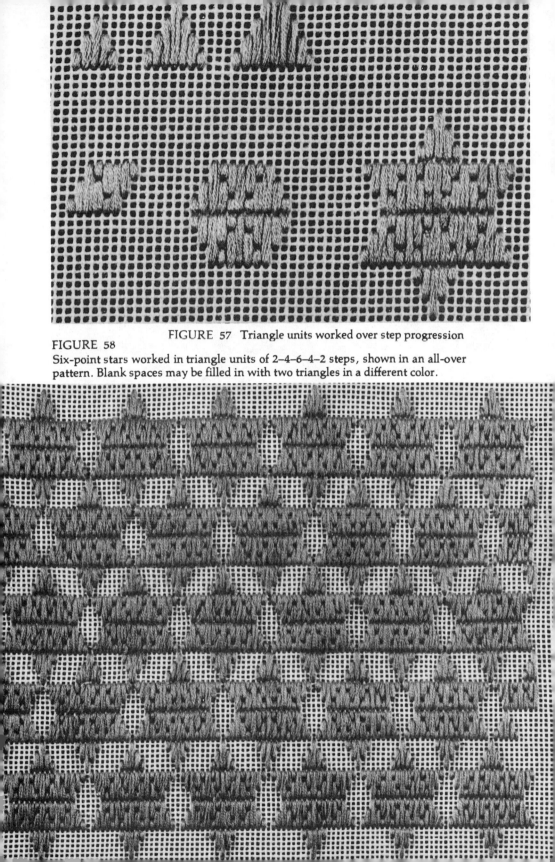

FIGURE 57 Triangle units worked over step progression

FIGURE 58
Six-point stars worked in triangle units of 2–4–6–4–2 steps, shown in an all-over pattern. Blank spaces may be filled in with two triangles in a different color.

Straight Cross Stitch Pattern

The Straight Cross Stitch pattern (Figure 59) is a small textured stitch pattern. It may be worked in diagonal, vertical, or horizontal lines on double-thread or single interlocked canvas.

In Figure 60 the Straight Cross Stitch is worked in diamond patterns on double-thread canvas and also between the canvas threads. Worked in this way it does not give any coverage but may be used to decorate a canvas and still leave the mesh open. It would look good as a window hanging.

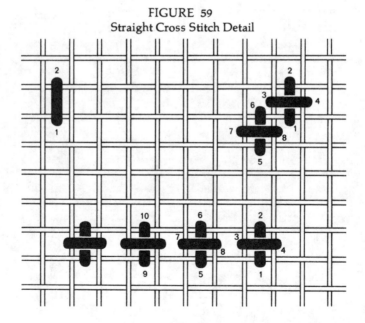

FIGURE 59
Straight Cross Stitch Detail

FIGURE 60
Straight Cross Stitch Pattern Variations

Double Paris Stitch Pattern

The Double Paris Stitch pattern (Figure 61) is worked like a Cross Stitch, but its texture is less rigid. In close formation it resembles the Brick Stitch texture, but it is much fuller and tighter. It consists of two vertical stitches worked over four canvas threads in the same mesh and a third stitch as a crossbar. The Double Paris may be worked in diagonal or horizontal rows (Figure 62) and is an excellent texture for rugs on # 5 canvas. Create bold diagonal or horizontal stripes for a stunning effect. (Figure 63.)

FIGURE 62
Double Paris Stitch Variations

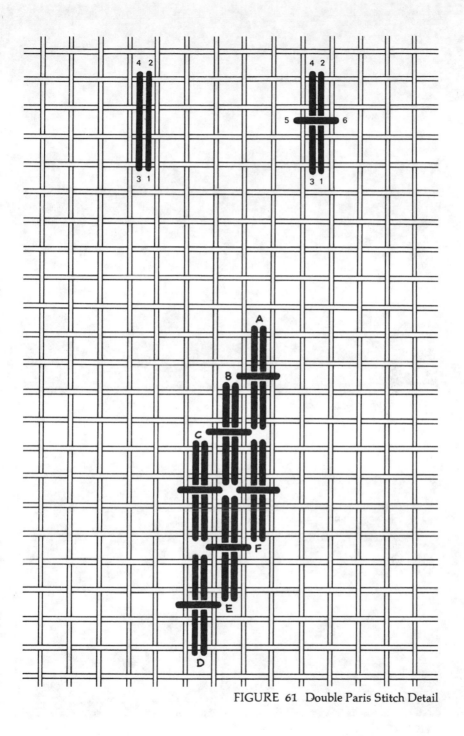

FIGURE 61 Double Paris Stitch Detail

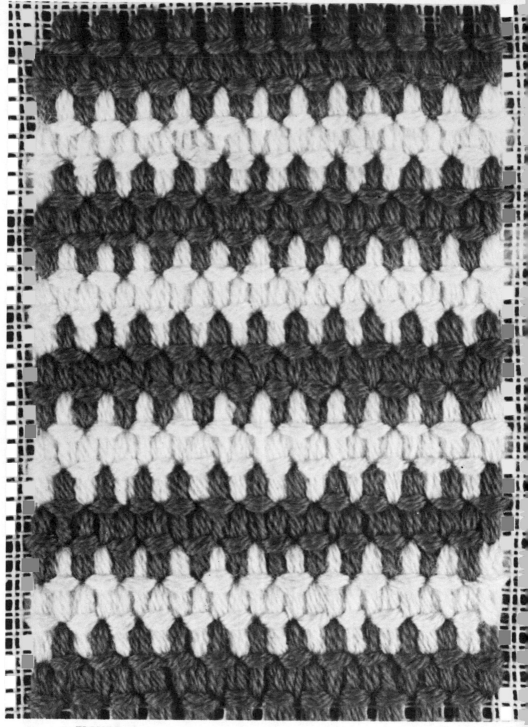

FIGURE 63
Double Paris Stitch worked as a rug texture on # 5 double-thread canvas with
two full strands Persian or one strand rug yarn.

Bargello—Linear Patterns

A linear Bargello pattern is a series of single and multiple sets of stitches in ascending and descending step formation. (Figures 64, 65, and 66.) The single steps are the diagonal line within the Brick Stitch framework, and the simplest linear pattern is a zigzag row of single steps over four canvas threads and under two. Single steps can be made longer by placing them over six canvas threads and under three.

Multiple sets of stitches are small groups of Straight Gobelin. Worked in combination with single steps, they form assorted curves that are also used as linear patterns.

A Bargello curve is illustrated in four steps in Figure 67. It begins with a single stitch over four canvas threads and ends with a set of four stitches in a row. It then descends to complete the curve. The size and depth of the curves depend on the number and length of stitches.

Another linear pattern is the onion dome or persimmon. (Figure 68.) It begins with the same formation as the curve, but when it reaches its widest step it decreases upward to one stitch which becomes the center point. The second half of the pattern is completed in reverse.

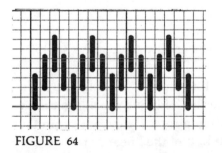

FIGURE 64

FIGURE 65 Zig-zag over four canvas threads and under two

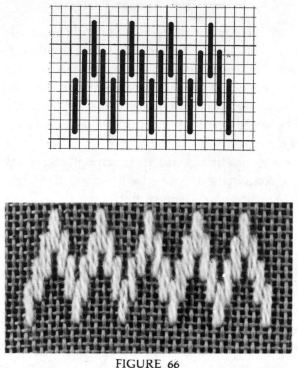

FIGURE 66
Zig-zag over six canvas threads and under three

Study the three basic linear patterns and work up a few samples in various gauges. See also Figure 69.

To create a linear pattern, a lead line must be established. Fold the square of canvas in half, crease the fold, and mark the center with a pin. Unfold canvas and, allowing for a 2" margin, begin the line at top center and work the first half of the linear pattern to the right margin. Return to the center point and work the second half to the left margin. The manner in which the pattern is centered depends on individual interpretation.

Once the lead line is established, begin a second line directly below it at one end and follow it step-by-step to the opposite end. Bargello may be worked from right to left or left to right.

Continue working the consecutive rows in selected colors. Color placement plays a very important part in linear Bargello design.

Top: A, Small Handbags (Figures 28 and 117); B, Four-way Geometric Design (Figure 104); C, Eyeglass Case worked in linear design with Double Brick Stitch Pattern (Figures 29 and 128); D, Soft Slippers (Figures 118–121). Bottom: 8-point Star Variations (Figures 109–114).

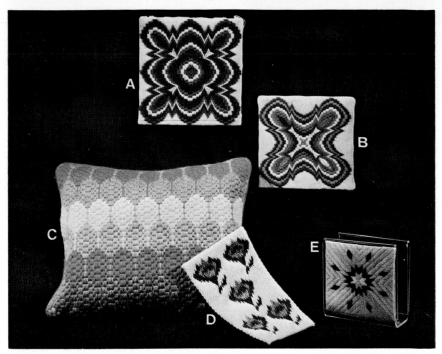

Top: A, 4-way Bargello as seen on cover (Figure 106); B, 4-way Bargello (Figure 107); C, Bargello Pillow; D, Carnations (Figures 33, 34, and 35); E, Letter Holder courtesy Toni Totes, Inc. showing 8-point Star (Figures 109–114). Bottom: A, Patchwork Bargello Design (Figures 115 and 116); B, Bargello Design with Triangles (Figure 54); C, Handbag courtesy Toni Totes, Inc. (Figures 24 and 25).

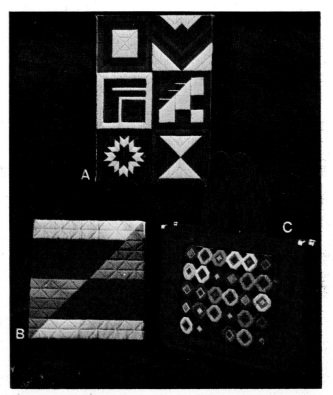

Top: 4-way Ribbon Bargello (Figures 102 and 103). Bottom: Belts (Figures 122–127).

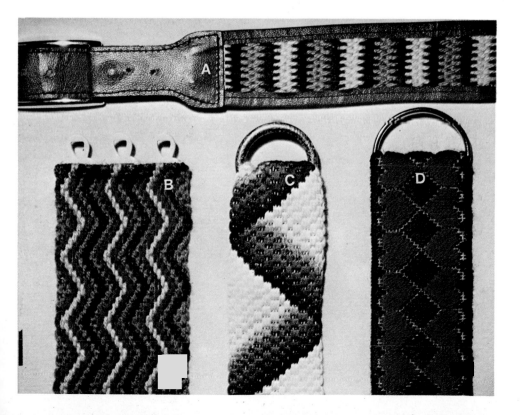

A, Angled Bargello (Figure 108); B, Doll House Rug worked in Brick Stitch Stripes (Figure 30).

Alternate contrasting colors or use a gradation of several shades in the same color family. In most good stores, needlepoint yarns are available in as many as eight graduated shades.

Place shades in lines of dark to light and repeat as often as the space allows. Or, reverse the color sequence for a "mirror image" effect by working dark to light and then light to dark.

Finish the top and bottom lines with compensating stitches. These are stitches that have to be shortened or adjusted to fit in odd places or to straighten out a margin line. (Figure 70.)

Figure 71 is a small pillow in single steps of 4 and 2 worked in five shades of blue. Figures 72, 73, and 74 show two more examples of linear Bargello design.

In addition to the evenly spaced Bargello steps of 4–2 and 6–3, Bargello designs are also created with long and short stitches. These are the foundation of the Flame Stitch patterns. Traditionally, the long stitches are placed over six canvas threads and the short ones over two threads. The work method is: over six, under one, over two, under one, and repeat—6–1–2–1. These stitches may also be worked in multiple sets as well as single steps.

FIGURE 67
Stitch progression for Bargello curves

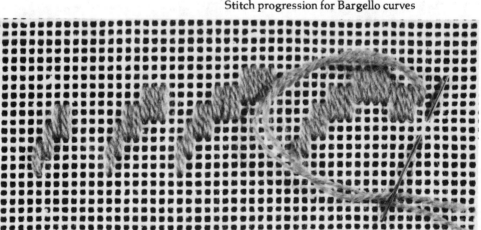

65

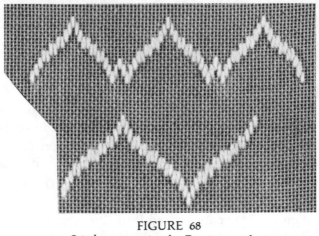

FIGURE 68
Stitch progression for Persimmon design

Figures 75 and 76 illustrate three Bargello patterns with long and short stitches. The rows of stitches alternate, with the short stitches placed over the long ones.

This technique requires a skilled hand and should be considered as an advanced project. Work stitches evenly and with special care. If the short stitches twist and show canvas, work them in two motions.

FIGURE 70
Finishing top and bottom lines with compensating stitches

FIGURE 69 Bargello curves and ovals

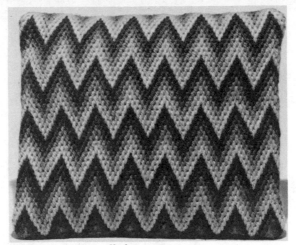

FIGURE 71 Bargello linear pattern

FIGURE 72 Linear Bargello design for Figure 74, A

FIGURE 73 Linear Bargello design for Figure 74, B

FIGURE 74 Stitch Detail for Linear Bargello design (see Figures 72 and 73)

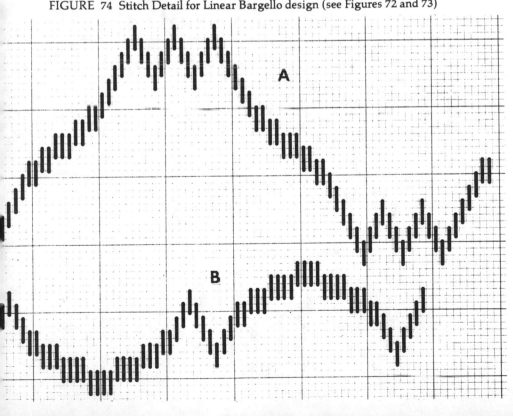

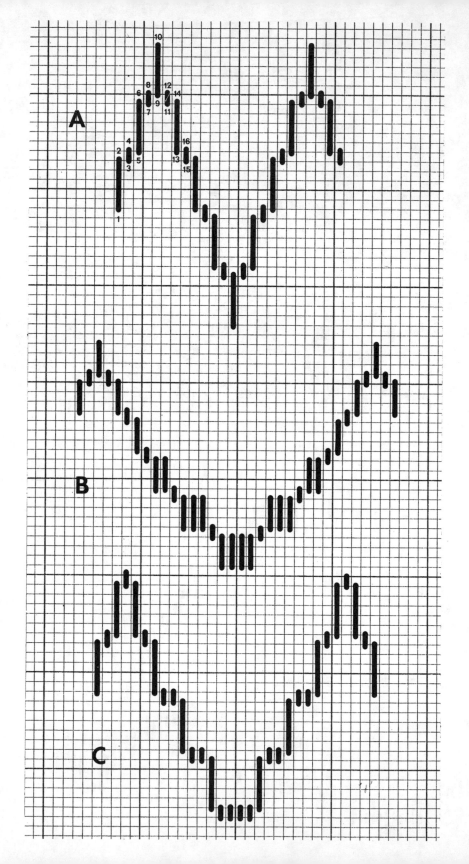

FIGURE 76
Bargello Long and Short Linear Designs
(see Figure 75, A, B, and C)

FIGURE 75
Stitch Detail for Bargello Long and Short Linear Designs
(see Figure 76, A, B, and C)

Bargello—Patterns and Design Outlines

Instead of following the lead line in a linear pattern, reverse the second line to form another pattern. The simplest is the diamond shape created from two reversed zigzag lines. (Figure 77.) The reverse line is shown in darker yarn to indicate the direction of stitches. Figures 78, 79, and 80 are variations of small patterns.

The small patterns may be filled with one or more colors and the larger ones with alternating colors or with small patterns as shown in Figure 81.

FIGURE 77
Diamond Shapes made from two reverse zig-zag lines (single steps)

FIGURE 79
Diamond Shapes made from
two reverse zig-zag lines
(double steps)

FIGURE 78
Diamond Shapes made from two reverse zig-zag lines (double steps)

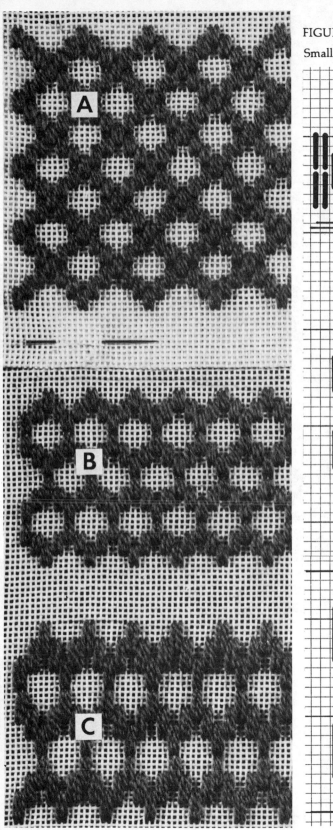

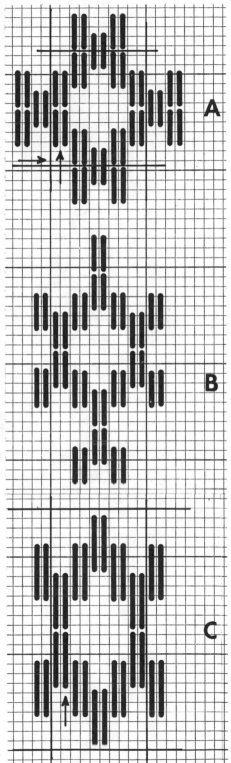

FIGURE 80
Small Diamond Pattern Variations

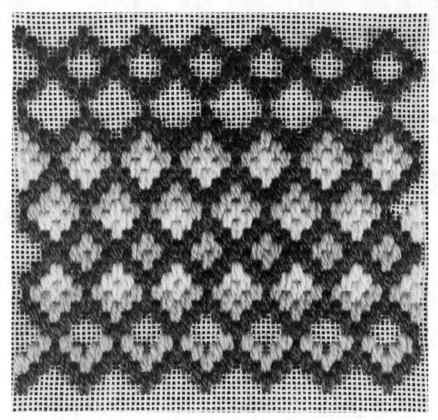

FIGURE 81
Small Diamond patterns filled in

Figures 82, 83, and 84 show a Bargello pattern based on the persimmon outline. The yarn colors graduate from light to dark. Work the linear pattern and reverse the line in alternating rows to form the open pattern. Complete the outlines first, and then fill with selected colors. Fill in one or two patterns as a guideline, and then fill the rest of the patterns.

FIGURE 82

Stitch Detail for Persimmons (see Figures 83 and 84)

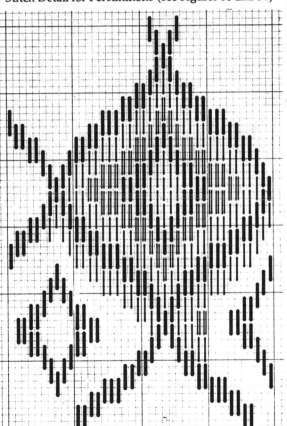

FIGURE 83
Persimmon patterns and progression

FIGURE 84
Small area rug worked in Persimmon pattern with alternating shades of color

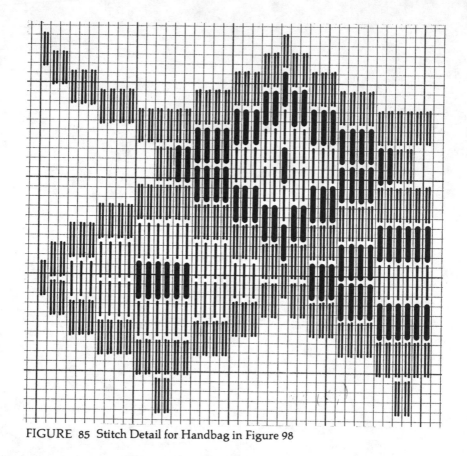

FIGURE 85 Stitch Detail for Handbag in Figure 98

FIGURE 86 Round pattern creates small diamond pattern in alternate rows

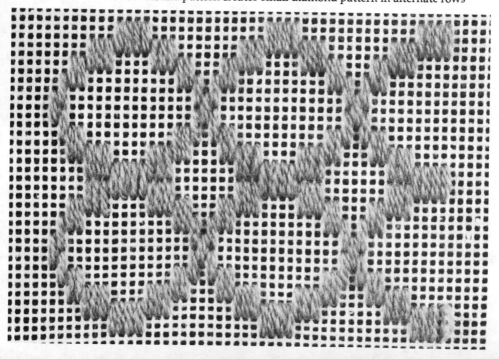

Round and oval patterns (Figure 86) create small diamond patterns in alternate rows as shown in the handbag in Figure 87.
These can be handled as separate patterns and filled in with different colors. (Figure 85.)

FIGURE 87
Handbag courtesy Toni Totes, Inc. (see List of Suppliers)

Depth Perception

Depth perception is an optical illusion created through the special placement of yarn colors. (Figure 88.)

Work the pattern outlines in the lightest value of one color family. Place the next five shades in a gradation of light to dark as shown in Figure 89. The remaining area is completed in two shades of a contrasting color. When seen from a distance, the pattern appears to have depth. Another design that creates a similar illusion is shown in Figures 90 and 91. It is worked in five shades of green.

Figure 92 is a sample of one large open pattern. This is a variation of the lemon pattern outline, and the stitches are worked over four canvas threads. What makes it large is the number of single and multiple stitch units. The design is worked in orange and brown, but any colors would be effective.

FIGURE 88
Depth perception within Persimmon pattern

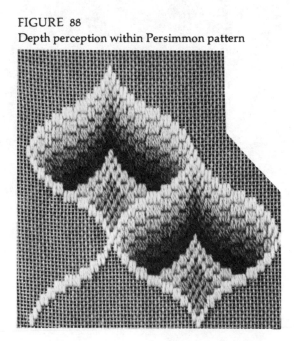

Study the graph in Figure 93 and work the center outline first. Finish one quarter of the pattern at a time. The center may be filled with a lovely needlepoint or a hand-painted picture without any stitchery. To create a smaller frame, place additional outlines into the inner framework.

Figure 94 shows an optical illusion based on the persimmon pattern. This large single pattern may be filled with alternating shades of light, medium, and dark. Create the largest complete pattern first to establish the over-all size of the design, and fill in the rest of the colors in diminishing inner outlines.

FIGURE 89
Depth perception progression

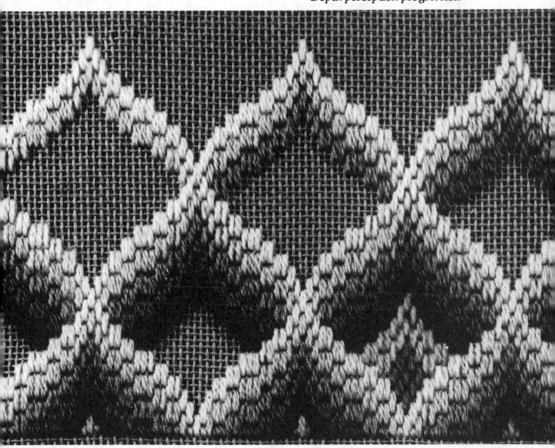

FIGURE 90 Depth perception within Diamond pattern

FIGURE 91 Depth perception progression

FIGURE 92
Large open Bargello pattern based on Persimmon outline

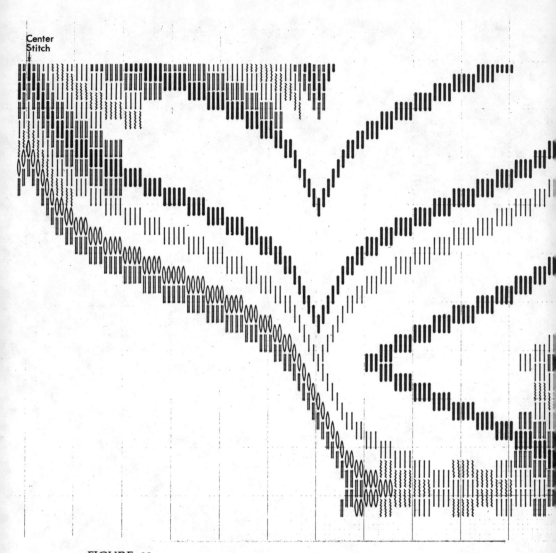

Center
Stitch

FIGURE 93
Stitch Detail for Figure 94

84

FIGURE 94
Optical Illusion based on Persimmon design outline

Mitered Bargello

Miter is a term borrowed from carpentry, where it refers to a joint made by fitting two pieces of wood into each other at a 45° angle. In Bargello stitchery, the Straight Gobelin Stitch which may be worked vertically as well as horizontally, creates a mitered effect when the two lines of stitches meet in the same canvas square and are perpendicular to each other.

Mitering is easy to learn. Begin by working up a row of Straight Gobelin Stitches in close formation. Diminish the width of the line by making the stitches shorter, one canvas thread at a time. (Figures 95 and 96.)

When the last stitch is placed over a single canvas thread, place the next stitch at right angles into the same canvas square and over one canvas thread. Continue working at right angles, increasing the length of each stitch by one canvas thread until the largest stitches meet at the end of the miter line. Finish the line of full stitches to the point where the next miter line is formed. The miter line should be very neat, with each mitered stitch meeting its counterpart in the same square on a diagonal line.

Miter lines are the foundation of eight-point stars and all the four-way Bargello designs.

FIGURE 95
Stitch Detail for Miter line

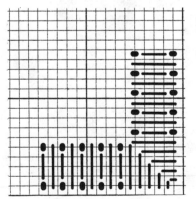

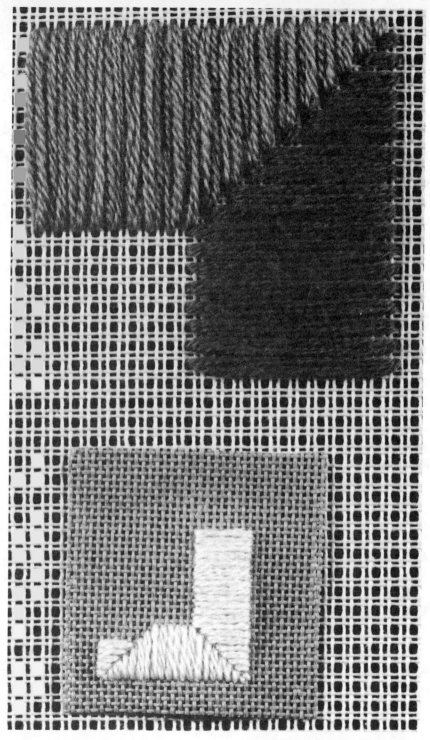

FIGURE 96 Mitering Bargello

Four-way Bargello

Once you learn to construct a simple miter line, practice with some of the conventional linear patterns. Any linear pattern can be mitered and worked four ways. The miter line must be very clear, however, or the design will look uneven.

A simple foolproof method of creating accurate four-way Bargello designs is to place a miter framework on the canvas before outlining the Bargello. To begin a four-way Bargello, work a large cross through the center of the canvas with Running Stitches carried diagonally through the canvas threads. (Figure 97.) Find the center of the canvas, thread a needle with a strand of yarn long enough to reach diagonally across it, and work the running stitches from the center to the lower left-hand corner, leaving only half the thread at the center point. Rethread the needle at the center point, and work the Running Stitches to the upper right-hand corner. Repeat with a second thread from center to the upper left and to the lower right. If you run the stitches from one corner across to the opposite one, the lines will not cross at dead center because the canvas strands are not perfectly square.

Study the two frameworks shown in Figure 97 and notice that one creates a single center where a design may end with four single stitches sharing one center mesh square. The other framework creates a double stitch center.

The proper framework to use will depend on the number of stitches in the center of the lead line. The framework is shown in bold dark threads for easy visibility, but it should actually be worked in a thread that is only slightly darker than the canvas. Once covered with Bargello stitches, the thread should not show through.

To create a four-way Bargello design, work up this framework first. A penciled diagonal line is not as accurate or as visible as a stitched line. Drag the point of a needle through the center of the framework. Mark the center point (single or double) at the top, and work a linear pattern between the stitched framework. Work one line beneath the other until you reach the point in the center. Place the end stitches into the framework line, mitering each consecutive line.

FIGURE 97

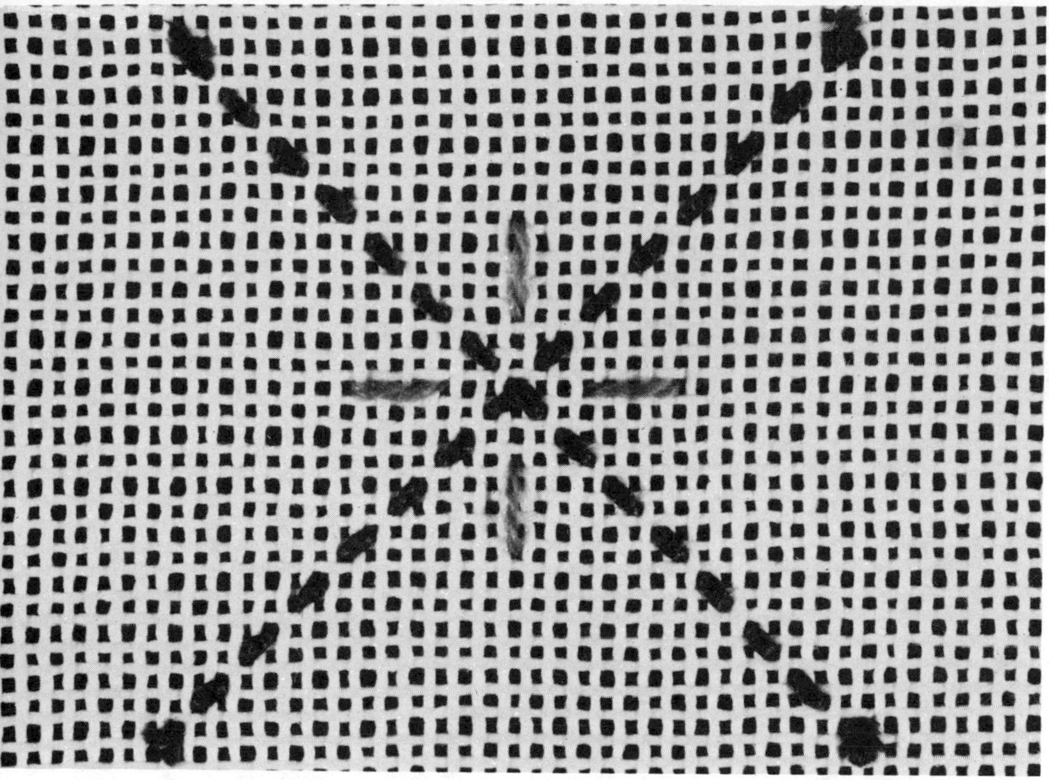

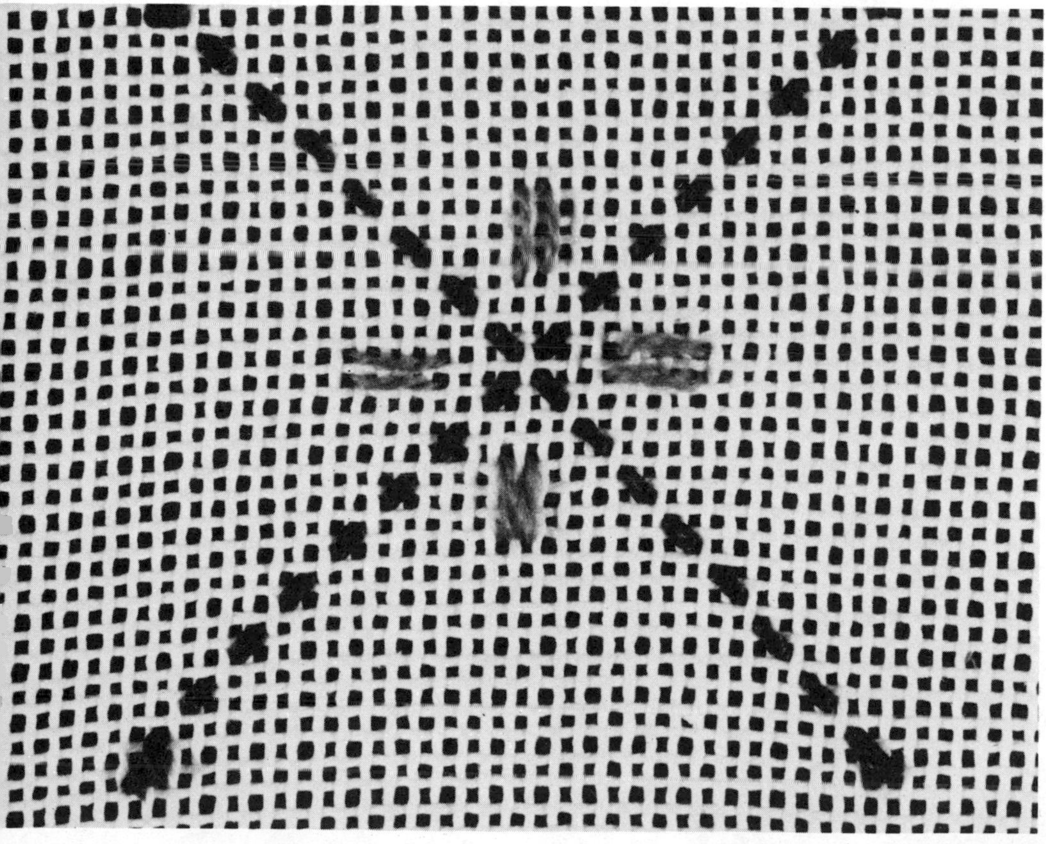

FIGURE 98   Four-way Bargello based on Carnation pattern

As the design develops, you will find that in most cases a stitch placed over a single canvas thread in a miter line does not show up well; it may be incorporated into the preceding line. This was done on the four-way Bargello on the cover. The miter lines in purple and yellow and the center green have omitted stitches over single canvas threads. The effect is very smooth and even.

Once a quarter pattern is established, turn the canvas once and complete the second quarter. Complete the rest of the design one quarter at a time, being very careful to work the miter lines evenly. The four-way Bargello designs in this book will illustrate a variety of possibilities.

Figure 98 is based on the Carnation pattern. This design is extremely effective when worked in three shades including a stark white. If you check back to Fig. 33, you will see the Carnation within the framework of the Brick Stitch texture.

FIGURE 99 Four-way Bargello based on Lemon pattern

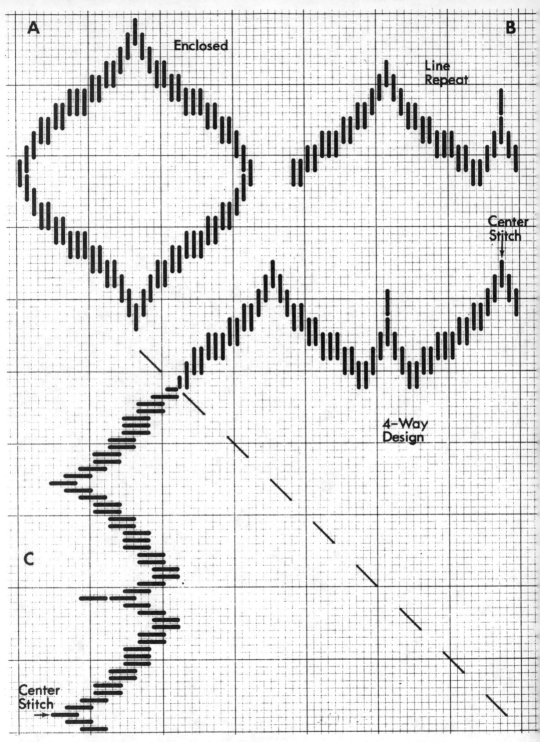

FIGURE 100 Stitch Detail for Figure 99

The design shown in Figures 99 and 100 is based on a four-way Lemon pattern outline. The design is a little fanciful, an effect created simply through color placement. The lemon outline is clearly visible.

Figure 101 is also based on a four-way Lemon pattern.

FIGURE 101

The design in Figures 102 and 103 represents a Ribbon pattern. This is an optical illusion achieved through color placement and shading. When the framework is in place, the design is worked along the sides and not into a center point. Study the design and you will see its resemblance to the Lemon pattern on page 92. Because of the nature of the ribbon design, the four sides are not the same but nevertheless have to be worked within a miter framework. Fill the remaining area with Half-Cross (Tent) Stitches and extend the background several inches so that the ribbon appears to be floating. This pattern may also be framed on blank canvas, in which case the miter framework should be taken out. (See color page C3.)

FIGURE 102

Ribbon Pattern based on a four-way Persimmon design outline (see color page C3, Top).

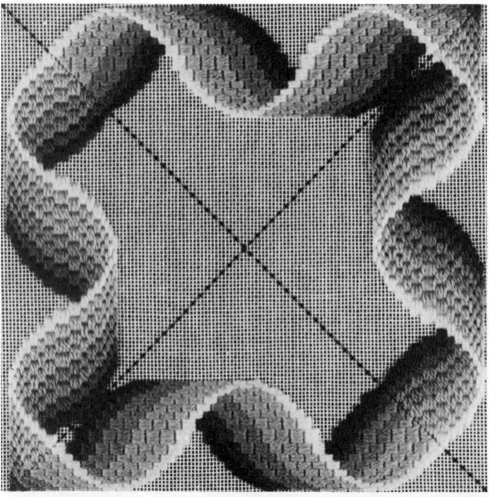

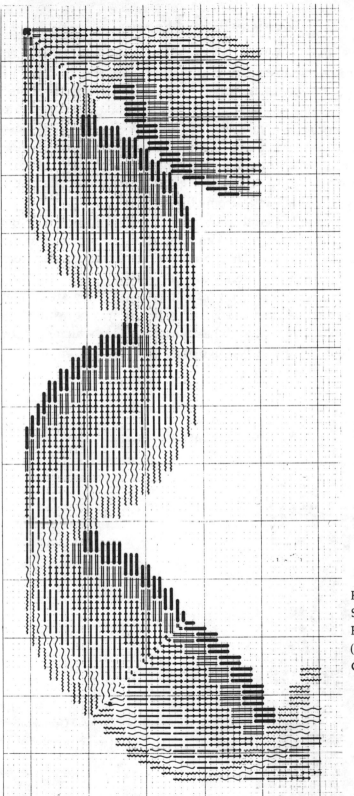

FIGURE 103
Stitch Detail for
Figure 102
(see color page
C3, Top)

95

Four-way Ribbed Pattern

Figure 104 is based on a geometric pattern. All rows are worked over three canvas threads. Begin at the top and work one row at a time, changing colors as indicated on the graph and color photograph. (See color page C1.) Thread each color onto a separate needle. If there is any yarn left and the color will appear close enough on a descending row, bring the threaded needle to the surface of the work and pin it on the canvas near at hand. (Figure 105.) Do not leave long threads dangling on the underside of the work. They will tangle and become fuzzy.

Work miter lines carefully, following the instructions on page 86. Finish design to the center point. Turn canvas once so that the finished quarter is on your left, and work the second quarter from the top. Finish all four quarters in the same way.

This pattern is worked on # 12 canvas with three strands of Persian-type yarn. Actual size is 16" × 16". It may be worked on larger mesh (such as # 5) with heavy rug yarn, in which case the stitches should be worked over five or six threads.

FIGURE 105
Working with alternating colors

FIGURE 104
Stitch Detail for Four-way Geometric Pattern
(see color page C1, Top, B)

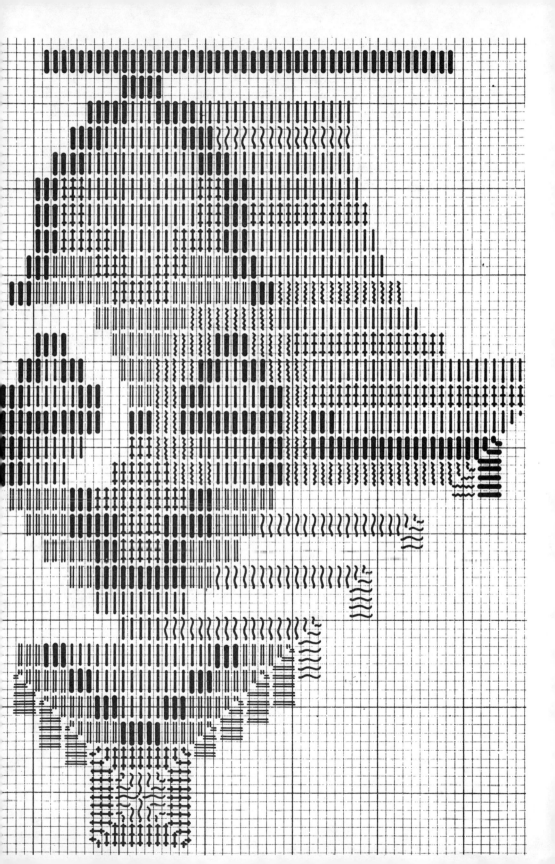

In order to estimate the amount of canvas needed for # 5, count the canvas threads (graph lines) from the center to the top and multiply by two. This will give you the total number of threads both horizontally and vertically (the design is square). Divide this total by 5 and allow a 3″ margin all around for folding back.

There are 92 canvas threads from top to center—multiplied by 2 this equals 184; $184 \div 5 = 37$ (rounded). Add a 3″ margin, and you will need a 40″ square of # 5 canvas to create a very handsome wall hanging.

The design in Figure 106 is based on the half round pattern outline. It may be left on unfinished canvas or filled in with a continuation of the four-way pattern in black or any of the colors in the design. (See front cover.)

Figure 107 shows a slight variation on this design, giving a larger pattern. (See color page C2)

Figure 108 is a four-way pattern. It is not mitered. The design consists of four triangles worked in Brick Stitch over two canvas threads. The stitches are all the same size. Each triangle is a repeat pattern and differs from the others in color placement only. (See color page C4.)

FIGURE 106
Four-way pattern based on half-round
Bargello design outline (see front cover)

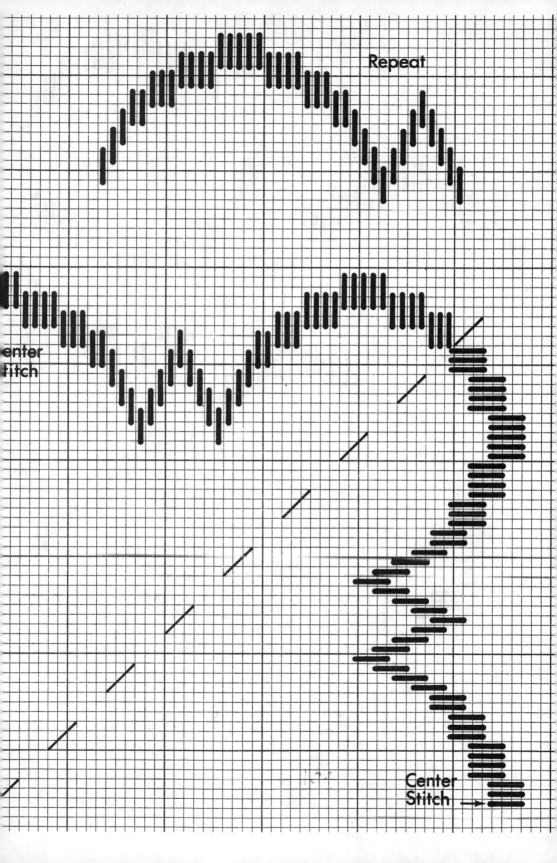

Repeat

Center
Stitch

Center
Stitch →

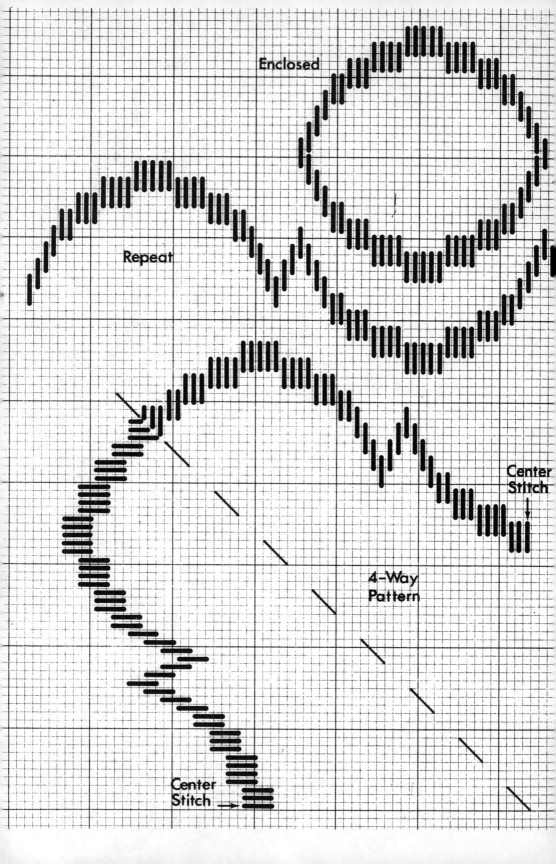

FIGURE 108
Four-way angled Bargello based on a Brick Stitch pattern (see color page C4, A)

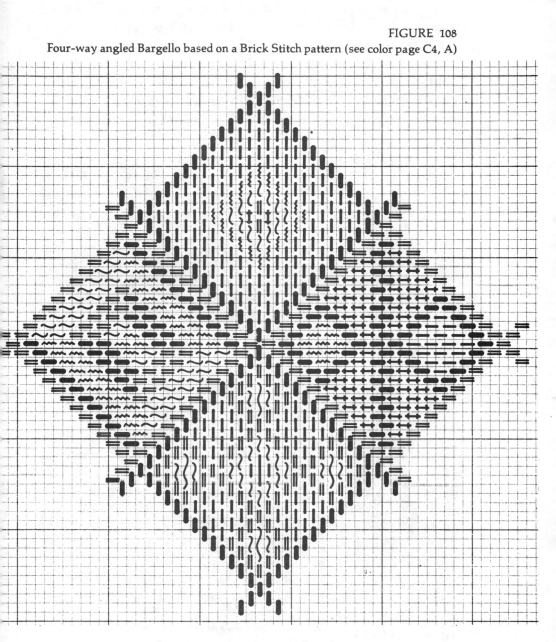

FIGURE 107
Four-way pattern variation (see color page C2, Top, B)

Eight-point Stars

Eight-point stars are worked in a four-way framework but are not mitered. They are based on the diagonal lines of the Straight Gobelin Stitches. Figure 109 is a step-by-step guide to construction of an eight-point star. The striking possibilities of this design are the result of color placement, as can be seen in the variations on color page C2. The design in pink and blue is a color variation of the stars in Figure 110. Two points are blue and two are pink.

FIGURE 110 (See color pages C1, Bottom, and C2, Top, E)

FIGURE 109
Step-by-step construction of an 8-point star
(see color pages C1, Bottom, and C2, Top, E)

For best results, colors should be worked in units of three or four stitches over five canvas threads. Star variations are unlimited—a few are shown in Figures 111, 112, and 113. Figure 114 shows the stitch detail for Figures 112 and 113.

FIGURE 111
8-point Star pattern variation (see color pages C1, Bottom, and C2, Top, E)

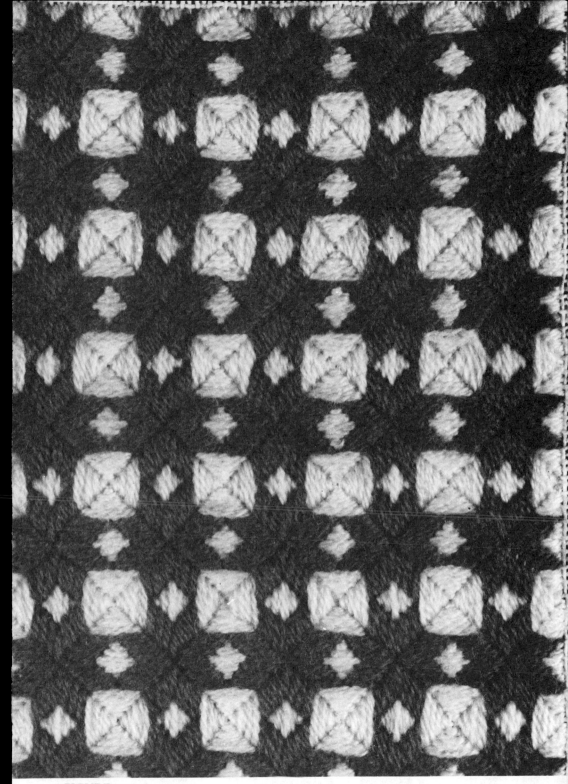

FIGURE 112
Same star pattern as Figure 116, worked in different colors (see color pages C1, Bottom, and C2, Top, E).

FIGURE 114
Stitch Detail for Figures 112 and 113
(see color pages C1, Bottom,
and C2, Top, E)

FIGURE 113
8-point Star Variation
(see color pages C1, Bottom,
and C2, Top, E)

The design shown in black and white in Figure 115, in color on page C2, and in graph outline in Figure 116, is an excellent project to try after you have mastered the eight-point star and mitering. This design works very well in primary or bold colors.

FIGURE 115
(See color page C2, Bottom, A)

PROJECTS

Handbag

(See color page C1.)

This very simple tote bag can be made in any size, but rectangle larger than 10" x 12" should be interlined with an extra piece of canvas or buckram.

MATERIALS: Two rectangles of worked Bargello with 2"
unworked margin
Two rectangles of lining fabric
Decorative cord or braid
Needles and matching thread

Finish and block both rectangles. Trim away any tape or selvage. (Figure 117, A.) Fold back the remaining margin, and miter each corner. (Figure 117, B.) Work a Running Stitch around the margin to fasten it to the worked canvas. These stitches should not show on the right side of the work. Press and miter lining pieces, place each against its canvas counterpart and stitch all around with thread to match the lining. (Figure 117, C.) Sew the lined rectangles together with right sides up. Stitch decorative cord or braid around the seams and the opening to cover canvas threads or work a row of close stitches as in the eyeglass case.

A strap or handle can be made with two lengths of decorative cord, a length of chain, or any other suitable material. (Figure 117, D.)

FIGURE 116
Stitch Detail for Figure 120 (see color page C2, Bottom, A)

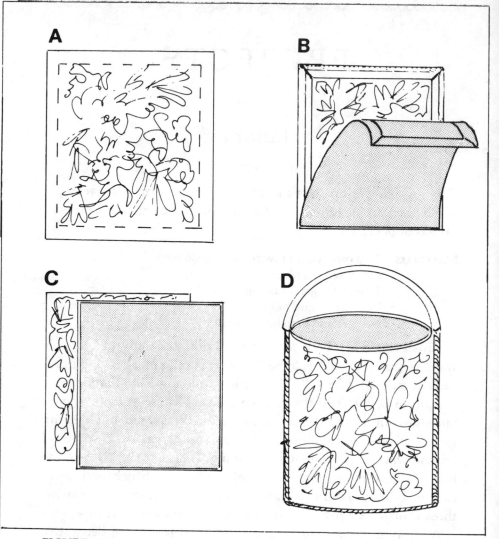

FIGURE 117
Step-by-step instructions for finishing small handbags (see color page C1, Top, A).

Soft Slippers

(See color page C1.)

MATERIALS: ¼ yd. # 12 interlocked mono canvas
¼ yd. felt for lining
Two small skeins each of magenta, turquoise, and orange
Persian-type yarn worked two ply
Sewing thread to match felt
Tapestry needle and sharp-pointed sewing needle
Sharp-pointed marking pen for outlines

Outline both feet on two sheets of paper, cut out, and use as patterns. Place these patterns lengthwise on the strip of canvas. Center the width and allow 3" margins at heel and toe. Outline paper pattern and the slipper pattern around it. (Figure 118, A.)

Draw the *T* between parallel canvas threads. This will be a cutting line. It is important to use interlocked canvas. (Figure 118, B.)

The slippers are cut like Indian moccasins and not like standard shoes. The line A-A measures 6" for a medium-sized slipper. The length of the slipper outline is equal to the length of the paper pattern of your foot plus 1" at each end. The rest is only margin allowance. The *T* bar is 3½" from the toe line. (Figure C.)

Outline the slippers on two pieces of canvas and then make two identical outlines on the felt. Outline the paper patterns of your feet on the felt and cut two of each foot. These will be used as the soles of the slippers.

The Bargello pattern is shown in graph outline in Figure 119 and photographically in Figure 120. It may need a minor adjustment to allow for size difference. Simply add a row or two as needed. Work Bargello pattern across the toe box and on either side of the *T* division line. Do not cross any yarn under the *T* line. The needlework covers the area A-A or the inner framework in Figure C. Work two slipper tops.

When needlework is completed, trim all thread ends and steam press. Allow it to dry, and then cut around the outline marked *x*. (Figure 118, C.) Cut through the *T* lines, being very careful to cut *between* the parallel canvas threads. The interlocking will not ravel at this point. Work a Running Stitch as indicated in Figure 118, C. Use a strong thread knotted at one end. Pull gently at the

111

other end of the thread to gather slightly and form a toe box. Manipulate the canvas with the fingers to even out the gathers. Fasten the thread securely.

Repeat this procedure with the felt patterns and then cut out the four soles. The slipper tops are identical and only the shapes of the soles will indicate which is right and which is left.

Turn the needlepoint slipper wrong-side out and line up A-A. (Figure 118, D.) Stitch to form the shape of the slipper. Pin a felt sole at toe and heel and baste all around. Machine stitch on the canvas side, catching at least one row of worked stitches. Trim canvas to 1/4". Turn slipper right-side out. Finish the other slipper up to this point. Check placement of soles for right and left.

Complete the felt linings in the same way, but don't turn them right-side out; slip them inside the needlepoint slippers. Be sure to line up the right and left soles with their counterparts. Line up the outer edges of the canvas and felt lining and work a row of close over-and-under stitches covering the cut canvas and the felt edge as you work. The finished slipper is shown in Figure 121.

Note: For best results, cut and baste a felt sample and try it on for size. Adjust if necessary, remove bastings, and use it as a pattern.

FIGURE 121
Finished Soft Slipper (see color page C1, Top, D)

FIGURE 118
Step-by-step instructions on finishing Soft Slippers

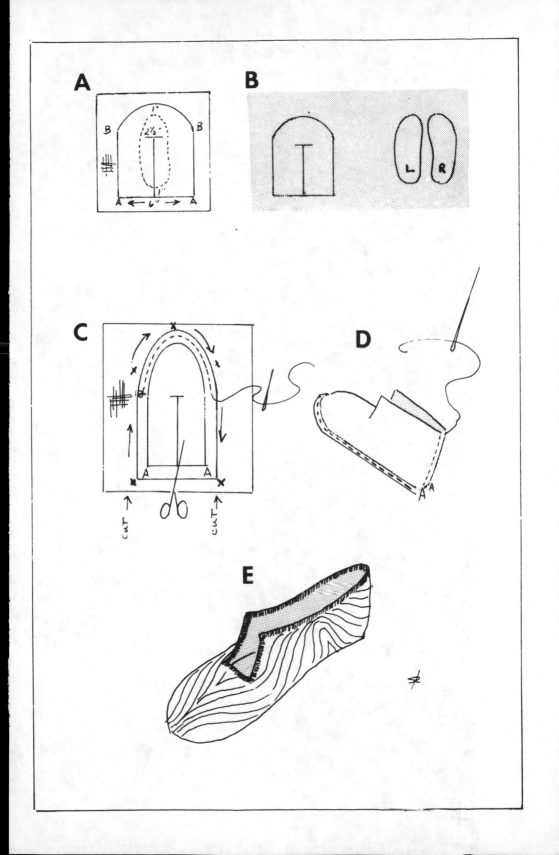

FIGURE 120
Finished Soft
Slipper top.
Cut through
center.

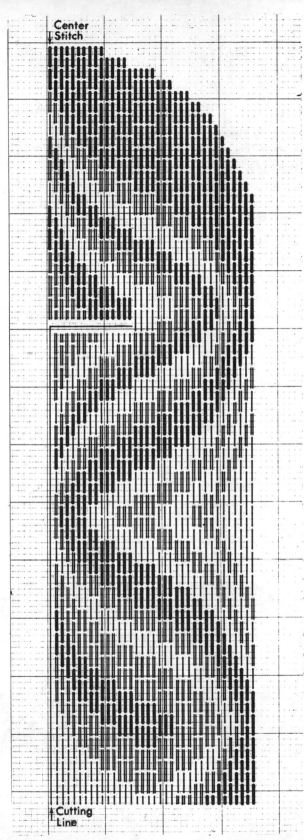

Center
Stitch

Cutting
Line

FIGURE 119
Stitch Detail for Soft
Slipper Bargello Pattern

115

Belts

(See color page C3.)

Select the pattern to be used on the belt from those shown in Figures 122, 123, 124, 125, and 126, and count the number of canvas threads it will require. Double this number and you will have the width of the belt. (Figure 127, A.)

Cut a strip of canvas to fit around your waist and add 4". Fold the long sides of the belt so that the edges meet in the center on the reverse side. (Figure 127, B.) Count again the number of threads on the right side, and adjust the fold if necessary to allow the number of threads needed for the pattern.

Work the Bargello design through both layers of canvas. (Figure 127, C.) The interlocked canvas is ideal for belts because it is light in weight and will not require taping. Finish the edges with over-and-under stitches. (Figure 127, D.)

When the needlework is completed, trim and tuck in yarn ends. Steam press over a damp towel and dry thoroughly.

Use a two-piece buckle, and attach each as indicated in Figure 127, E. Fold back enough of the excess length to allow a comfortable fit. Do not use the type of buckle that requires cutting eyelet holes into the needlework. Pre-finished belt kits are available in leather or plastic, complete with buckle and an insert of canvas ready for needlepoint. (See list of Suppliers.)

It is not necessary to line needlepoint belts because it only adds extra bulk to the waistline.

FIGURE 122
Belt Ribbon Pattern (see color page C3, Bottom)

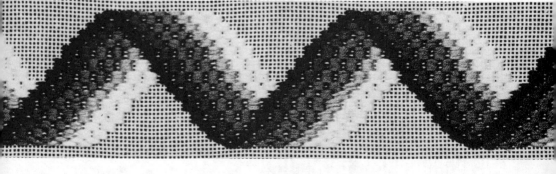

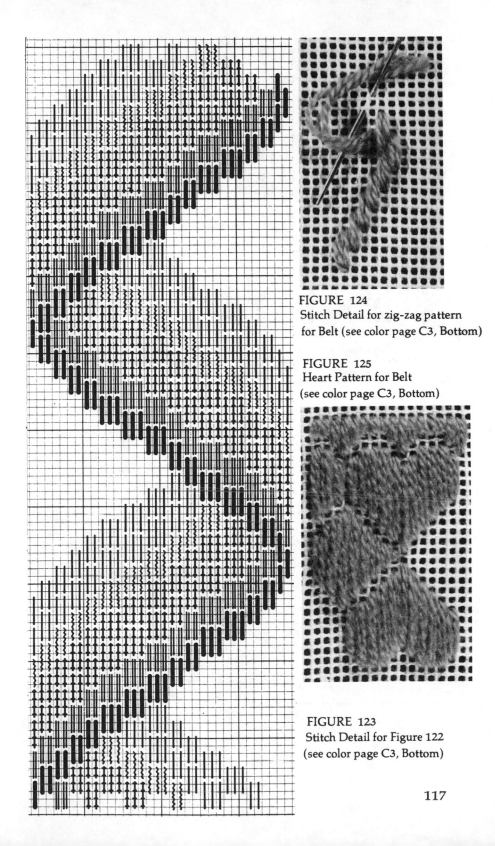

FIGURE 124
Stitch Detail for zig-zag pattern
for Belt (see color page C3, Bottom)

FIGURE 125
Heart Pattern for Belt
(see color page C3, Bottom)

FIGURE 123
Stitch Detail for Figure 122
(see color page C3, Bottom)

117

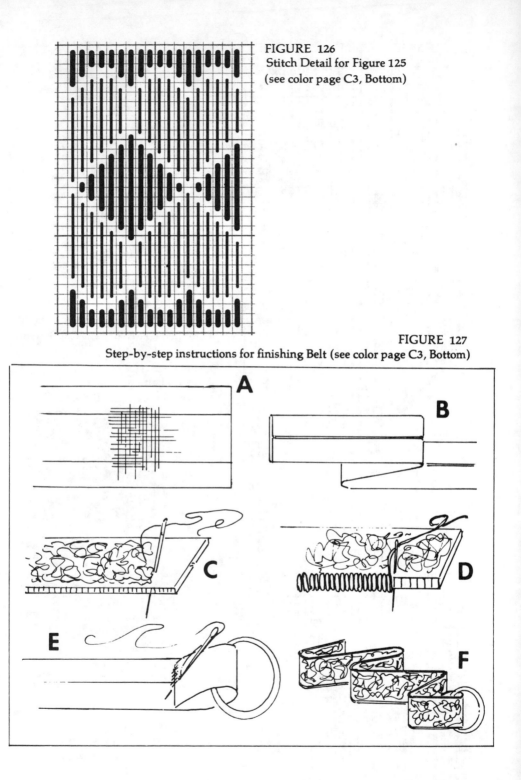

FIGURE 126
Stitch Detail for Figure 125
(see color page C3, Bottom)

FIGURE 127
Step-by-step instructions for finishing Belt (see color page C3, Bottom)

Eyeglass Case

(See color page C1.)

MATERIAL: # 12 interlocked canvas
            Lining (velveteen, satin, or other fabric)
            Yarn
            Tapestry needle and crewel needle

Measure and cut lining to fit glasses (Figure 128, A) allowing a 1/2" margin all around. Fold over, pin along the side, and slip in the eyeglasses. The glasses should slide easily in and out of the lining case. Remove pins and press flat.

Cut canvas square the same size as lining, allowing a 2" margin all around.

FIGURE 128
Step-by-step instructions for finishing Eye glass Case
(see color page C1, Top, C)

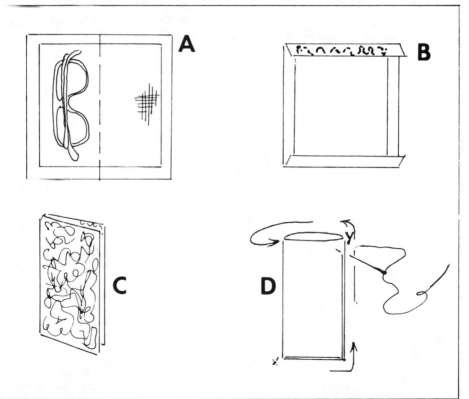

Tape the cut edges and work your favorite Bargello pattern within the margins. Stitches should not exceed a length of four canvas threads. Keep thread ends neatly trimmed. Steam on the wrong side and cut away the taped portion of the canvas, leaving about 1" unworked margin all around. Cut away any selvage.

Fold back the margin (Figure 128, B) and stitch it down all around with small Running Stitches or Back Stitches that fasten the fold to the worked canvas but do not show on the right side. Press over a damp towel and let dry. Fold back margins on the lining and press to crease the folds. Place lining against finished Bargello, with wrong sides together, and stitch all around the edges.

Fold the lined square in half, right-side out. (Figure 128, C.) Beginning at point x in Figure 128, D, sew the bottom and sides together to point y. Stitch around opening as indicated by arrows and finish at point y. Work small even stitches with two-ply yarn in a matching or contrasting color over and under the canvas edges. Use a sharp-pointed crewel needle, and place stitches close enough to cover all visible canvas threads.

FINISHING
AND MOUNTING
NEEDLEWORK

Needlework should be mounted as attractively as possible. Finished needlework can be handled like fabric and made into anything from pin cushions and eyeglass cases to impressive wall hangings and rugs.

In most cases, finishing and mounting should be handled by a professional who has the necessary skill and equipment for the job. The simple instructions included here are for finishing a few articles that can be handled by the beginner.

Blocking Needlework

All needlework should be blocked after completion. Blocking not only straightens distorted canvas, but also freshens the yarn and makes the stitches look more smooth and even.

There are several methods of blocking needlework; the best one depends on the fabric and stitches used. Vertical and horizontal stitches do not distort fabric and therefore do not require extensive blocking. A light steaming should be sufficient.

Place the finished work face-down on a cloth-covered board. Wring out a wet terry cloth towel and place it over the needlework. Glide a hot iron lightly over the towel—do not press down—until the towel stops steaming. Remove the towel, and while the canvas is still limp, turn it right-side up. Pull gently at the corners to square the canvas, then pin it down with push pins around the unworked margin. Let it dry for several hours.

If the work is uneven or if the canvas threads have been pulled too tightly, a water soaking is sometimes helpful. Assuming the canvas is not marked with water-soluble paints, soak the entire canvas in cool water to which a little Woolite or some Ivory soap flakes have been added.

Soak the work for several hours, roll it in a heavy towel to absorb the excess moisture, unroll it, and pin it face-side up as described above. Dry overnight. Bargello should not be stretched too much but gently pulled into shape. Do not soak anything but the best quality vat-dyed wool yarn.

Blocking needlework face-side up is preferable because one can see the stitches and avoid overstretching.

Framing Needlework

Needlework cannot be framed like a photograph or poster, nor should it be glued to a board. For best results, it must be stretched on a frame.

The best frame for needlework is the simple, sturdy artist's frame. These frames are sold in individual strips of 6" and up. Each end of the strip is grooved and mitered for easy assembly.

After a needlework has been stretched on an artist's frame, it can be slipped into a decorative frame. These frames are sold in packages of prefinished strips of one length. Since frame sizes are somewhat limited, check the supply of ready-made frames in your area before deciding on the design and dimensions of your needlework.

Once the frames have been selected, finish and block the needlepoint. Assemble the artist's frame, steam the needlepoint to relax the canvas (see blocking information), and place it over the frame. The worked area should not extend over the edge of the frame.

Place a few push pins into the corners and around the sides to keep the canvas from shifting. Fold the unworked margin of canvas over the edge of the frame and staple the center point on each side of the frame. The rows of stitches should look straight and the needlework smooth and even. Be careful not to overstretch.

Staple all around the frame, folding corners neatly as shown in Figure 129. If the staples protrude slightly, hammer them in. If a professional stapler is not available, use carpet tacks placed ¼″ apart.

Cut the canvas along the edges and place the finished piece in a decorative frame. Do not place glass over the needlework unless you are framing a fragile antique; and in that case, have a professional do the job. Antique frames can be used for needlework if they are deep enough to accommodate the artist's frame. A frame that was used for an oil painting is more suitable than one used for a photograph. Custom frames should aways be handled by a professional.

Note: The edge of the decorative frame should cover one or two rows of stitched canvas all around. Allow for it in the preliminary planning of the needlepoint.

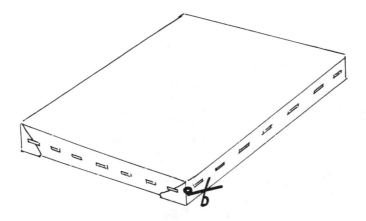

FIGURE 129
Stretching canvas on artist's frame

How To Make a Pillow

The loviest pillows are usually the simplest to make. They show off the stitchery with a minimum of frills and ruffles.

MATERIALS: Fabric backing in the same size and approximate weight as the needlework (velvet, duck, upholstery fabric, etc.)
Pillow filler, 1" larger than the dimension of needlework (dacron polyester or feathers and down—both available ready-made in department stores)
Decorative twisted cord or braid (optional)

Press fabric and pin to needlework with right sides together. Stitch several rows of large basting (Running) stitches across the entire width of the two fabrics at 2" intervals. These basting stitches will keep both fabrics flat and even.

Remove pins, and machine stitch on the needlepoint side as indicated in diagram outline. Two rows of machine stitches sewn at the lowest setting are better than one row of little stitches.

FIGURE 130   How to Make a Pillow

Clip corners at points, and remove basting threads. Turn pillow right-side out. Poke out the corners with your fingers.

Measure the entire outline of the pillow, and cut a length of cord or braid 1" longer. Don't stretch the cord while measuring. Tie a piece of thread close to the cut edges to prevent the cord from separating. (Figure 130.)

Beginning at the open end, pin the cord along the edge of the pillow to cover the machine stitching. Take small stitches in matching thread and stop at the other end of the pillow opening. Secure the cord at that point with an extra stitch, and remove needle. Finish the cord after the pillow is stuffed.

To stuff pillow, push a cotton ball into each corner, then insert the pillow filler. Fold the filler in half, slip it into the opening, and unfold it inside the casing. Hand stitch the opening closed by folding the needlework and fabric backing into the opening and lining up the edge with the existing machine stitching.

Rethread the needle on the decorative cord and stitch it over and closed edge. Overlap the end pieces of the cord, and tie the remaining thread over the two to keep them from unravelling. End with a few stitches.

Note: The opening and the ends of the decorative cord should be placed at the bottom line of the pillow. Check the needlepoint design before basting the outline.

LIST OF SUPPLIERS

Retail Only

La Stitcherie
72 Middle Neck Road
Great Neck, New York 11021

Canvas, yarn, kits, custom designs

Wholesale and Retail

Toni Toes of Vermont, Inc.
Route 100
South Londonderry, Vermont 05155

Handbags, kits for tennis racquet covers, belts for needlepoint, plastic enclosures
Will send catalogue

Walbead, Inc.
38 West 37th Street
New York, New York 10018

Beads, sequins, macrame
Will send catalogue

Wholesale Only

Paternayan Brothers, Inc.
312 East 95th Street
New York, New York 10028

Paternayan Persian yarn, canvas and needles, rug and crewel yarns, Rya cloth

Craft Yarns of Rhode Island
P.O. Box 151
Harrisville, R.I.

Three-ply Persian-type yarn, quick-point yarn, needlepoint canvas

Coats and Clark's
P.O. Box 1966
Stamford, Connecticut 06904

Cotton and rayon embroidery threads and rug yarns, craft yarns (acrylic washable), acrylic Persian-type yarn, needles

Handwork Tapestries
114 B Allen Blvd.
Farmingdale, New York 11735

Persian-type yarn, Laine Colbert three-ply tapestry yarn, Colbert six, French silk, canvas

Art Needlework Treasure Trove
P.O. Box 2440
Grand Central Station
New York, New York 10017

Canvas, yarns, linens, embroidery fabrics, and supplies

Howard Needlework Supply Co., Inc.
919 Third Avenue
New York, New York 10022

Canvas and embroidery fabric in linen, cotton, and polyester

William E. Wright Co.
One Penn Plaza
New York, New York 10001

Lace

E.T. Group Ltd.
230 Fifth Avenue
New York, New York 10017

Paternayan yarns, Alice Peterson painted canvases, Rya cloth

George Wells
The Ruggery
Cedar Swamp Road
Glen Head, New York 11545

Rug yarns, linen and Rya cloth, undyed yarn, special dyes for wool yarns, Hectograph pencils

Astor Place Ltd.
260 Main Avenue
Stirling, New Jersey 07980

Painted canvases and packaged kits

Cute and Custom
1A Munson Court
Melville, New York 11746

Painted canvases and packaged kits

Needlepoint U.S.A.
37 West 57th Street
New York, New York 10019

Painted canvases and packaged kits

Note: For all inquiries to dealers, enclose a self-addressed stamped envelope.